Altered Style

Sewing & Embellishing Wearable Fashions

Stephanie Kimura

©2008 Stephanie Kimura

Published by

kp **krause publications**
An Imprint of F+W Publications

700 East State Street • Iola, WI 54990-0001
715-445-2214 • 888-457-2873
www.krausebooks.com

Our toll-free number to place an order or obtain
a free catalog is (800) 258-0929.

The following trademarked terms and companies appear in this publication:
Clover, Fabri-Tac®, Dritz® Fray Check, Lycra®, Magna-Tac®, Q-tip®, Spandex, Teflon®, Velcro®

Library of Congress Control Number: 2007924849
ISBN-13: 978-0-89689-600-0
ISBN-10: 0-89689-600-5

Model shots by Photography by JD, Clintonville, WI
Designed by Heidi Bittner-Zastrow
Edited by Erica Swanson
Printed in China

Acknowlegments

I hope you'll check out thrift and consignment shops or look at the clothes you have and alter them with your unique style. Make a statement and dare to be different! Tell the world who you are instead of blending into cookie cutter fashions. All the Resource companies and people listed below are waiting to see your Altered Style!

I would like to thank Erica Swanson, my editor extraordinaire; Candy Wiza, acquisitions editor, who took a chance; and the incredible team of book designer Heidi Zastrow and photographers Kris Kandler and Bob Best at Krause Publications. They do their work in the quiet little town of Iola, Wisconsin. I would also like to thank J.D., Jean and Dave Wacker of Photography by J.D. in Clintonville, WI, along with the lovely models who made my projects sing: Amanda, Sussanah, Rebecca, Karen, Kylie and Nicole.

This book is dedicated to Edith (my mother, who knew I would love to sew because I carved my initials on her sewing machine cabinet as soon as I learned my abc's).

The companies listed on the Resource list made the creation of these projects possible. There are more companies, stores and friends to thank, and they are listed on my Web site. I would like to thank the organizations that create venues to keep sewing, quilting and crafting alive and well. Most of all, I want to thank all the creative sewers, quilters and crafters who support our industry.

Contents

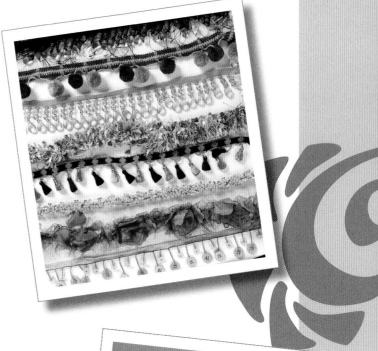

Something Borrowed

Something Blue

I Do!

Introduction

Altered style is all about adding your personal stamp and thoughts to everything in your life. Once you start, your life will never be the same again. You're probably already doing it unconsciously in a practical sense, so now use it creatively and meaningfully. "Altered Style" will lead to an enhanced lifestyle. You'll look at everything differently. No longer will shopping be humdrum, deciding between the black leather shoes that will match all the other black accessories or brown because it might be the new black…but you're not sure. No longer will you have to have the very latest and most costly styles. You'll learn to shop in your own closet, a friend's closet, consignment stores, thrift shops and sale racks.

Replace old buttons, change the shapes of collars and cuffs with lace, add grommets as embellishment and sprinkle sparkling crystals everywhere. Subtly add your secret thoughts to the inside of shoes and belts, or proudly blaze words across the shoulders of a jacket for all to see.

Check out magazines for the latest design ideas, and create your own version from the clothes you already have. Add snippets of vivid fabrics and exotic beads in hues you love. Use random shapes and a spontaneous placement method to create an abstract style. Use the element of surprise and impromptu doodling in the most unexpected places. You'll be surprised at how confident and fearless you'll feel! Wear these significant pieces of wearable art when you need to go out and conquer the world. Then, on days of quiet solitude and introspective peace, let the colors and artful images speak in nuances as the designs are placed in a purposeful trail across a vest. Add a cutout circle portal; the viewer will follow the path of textures and approach the round window that provides a glimpse into the artist's soul. Journal life's meaning encrypted in Haiku on vintage kimono fabric with a permanent marker. Use fabric adhesive, and bond it to the inside of the garment. These exercises in developing techniques will boost your self esteem when you begin to express yourself. You may even want to share your wearable art with others in a gallery setting!

To create something new, accessorize and add flourishes to projects made from the ingenious circle. Stretch the creative, problem-solving portion of your mind by thinking of ways to alter the circle to suit your needs. With just a folding of fabric, a few measurements and a simple equation, you will be able to create aprons, skirts, collars, cuffs, pockets and artful designs. Use these simple projects as a backdrop for the drop-dead gorgeous accessories you create.

Some days are just for silliness and frivolity: no worlds to conquer and no world needs to ponder, no techniques to learn and no equations to remember. Grab a pair of high-top sneakers and a handful of scrapbook supplies. No one said memories had to go in a book — and wouldn't it be fun to send them to your older sister….the accountant?

Getting Started

This book will be your BFF (best friend forever). We'll have fun, we won't watch the time, we'll spread everything out so we can see it all in a glance, we'll take chances, and we'll create our own style. Collect some specialty reference books as well as some excellent Web sites. There is a vast world of information about sewing machine needles, thread, seams and more, as well as the material found in your sewing machine manual.

There is some information about sewing...no, not rules, but the standard (for now). Some information is good forever, like basic sewing skills. Some information needs to be updated, such as new improved sewing notions. And some information applies to personal taste, like whether you should baste everything before sewing. Set your own standard to accommodate your skill level while you evolve. Take classes at a nearby shop, and add new techniques to your repertoire at your own pace.

Products

Some basic information on fabrics, stabilizers and notions is provided. Use this as a starting point, and update with new information as you go along. Get a three-ring binder and divide it into sections. Keep notes on the information you gather from reference books and Web sites (so you can go back and look it up in detail), save pages from sewing magazines (they explain the latest products), and sketch ideas for the future.

Fabrics

A trip to the fabric store can be overwhelming (in a good way!). Quilt stores are great because you can buy a lot of cotton fat quarters, sustenance for the altered soul. Buy in groups of four — it's only a yard! Select a main motif and supporting fabrics. Keep a stash of basic "tone-on-tones" to bridge all the prints. Always keep some black, white and red (or your favorite color). Yellow or a color with yellow mixed in (i.e. green or orange) adds zing.

When you are buying fashion fabric for the circle projects in this book, consider the drape, stretch and ravel factor. A heavier, woven fabric (such as denim or linen) will drape away from the body, creating a lovely fullness. A softer or loosely woven fabric (like chiffon or gauze) will fall close to the body. Knits usually fall close to the body. Fabrics like chiffon and knits allow you to add fullness with gathers with elegance, not poofiness.

How much stretch do you need, and why? Woven fabrics only stretch on the bias. When a circle is cut, there is minimal stretch in certain parts of the circle. This is great for aprons, wrap skirts, and skirts that will have a zipper and waistband. This is ideal for areas that require a finite measurement. A skirt with an elastic waistband will require a circle measurement of whichever is larger, the waist or hips. If the hips are larger, the waistband will have gathers.

When a circle is cut from a fabric such as chiffon, rayon, silk or a knit with two-way stretch, there is a lot of stretch. This is ideal for a smooth waist area and will accommodate any size hip with minimal gathering. The chiffon waistband will still need to be the largest measurement, but the chiffon will ease back with very little gathering. With a knit waistband that will stretch, the measurement will be somewhere between the smallest and largest measurement, depending on the stretch. When attaching the waistband to the skirt, use a narrow zigzag stitch to accommodate the stretch. There isn't a finite formula, so a little trial and error is required on an individual basis.

The ravel factor has always been a concern. Until now, all hems were finished in some manner. It was a standard and unbroken rule. Today, hemlines do not have to be finished if they do not ravel. This revolution began with casual clothing and now is evident with elegant evening wear. Embrace this groundbreaking revolution of altered style!

Leather and faux leather are great materials for complete projects, appliqués, straps on purses, closures and fringe. It doesn't ravel, and the edges do not have to be finished. Leather can be purchased as complete hides, in belt kits, and in strips as lacing. Faux leather is readily available in home decorating fabric departments with a 60" width.

When designing with existing clothing, consider the following things:

1 Does the garment fit well? If not, incorporate the fitting alterations into the design, or cut it up to make an accessory.

2 Are the colors pleasing? If not, embellish with a color scheme of fabric, beads, ribbon and crystals.

3 Is there space to add embellishment? If not, splice into the garment and add a panel of fabric or leather to embellish.

4 Does the garment have a pleasing design? If it does, consider just adding some sparkling crystals.

5 Does the piece already have unusual qualities? Look for denim jeans with intricate embroideries, interesting pockets, opportune rips and frays, authentic metal rivets, over dye in unusual shades, zippered pockets and button front plackets to create altered style.

Tip:
If the waistband is cut on the bias of woven fabric, it too will stretch. Ahh, the magic of bias!

Use leather for a professional finish.

Choose jackets with grommets and interesting pockets for a completely altered style!

Stabilizers

Stabilizers have transformed our lives. With the advent of machine embroidery, stabilizers have improved in quality and convenience.

Tear Away

These stabilizers are somewhat crisp, non-woven, and are removed after sewing. A shorter stitch length allows for easier removal. If that is not possible, place your finger on one side of the stitch and use your other hand to tear it away. This will keep you from pulling at the stitching. This stabilizer is available in convenient light, medium and heavy weights. You may want to begin with the lightweight version and add layers when more stabilization is required.

Leave In

These stabilizers are soft and remain part of the garment. They are available in several weights and colors.

Wash Away

These stabilizers are non-woven and designed to wash away after stitching. Most of the stabilizer can be removed by outlining the area with a wet Q-tip. They are available in a clear, plastic-like film, or as mesh and water-soluble paper-like sheets.

Spray On

This stabilizer is sprayed on to one side and ironed on the other side to allow permeation. This stiffens the fabric and washes out.

Adhesives

Adhesives can simplify your life and make sewing more enjoyable.

Spray On

Spray adhesives are convenient and available in pump and aerosol form. Many are task specific, providing temporary hold, permanent hold, quick fast-tack, and basting spray that allow pieces to be "repositioned". Be sure to use in a well-ventilated area and spray on a protected surface.

Fabric Glue

Fabric glue offers a quick grab and permanent bond. A wide variety is available for no-sew projects (applying rhinestones), for washable projects and for stretchable fabrics.

Fusible Web

This is a heat-set bonding agent. It is available in sheets, strips, with or without release paper, and with pressure-sensitive adhesive to keep in place temporarily.

Doubled-sided Tape

Clear, double-sided tape can be used for an instant permanent bond. It is available on a roll, in sheets, and die-cut in popular shapes. Cut to shape or length, remove the clear release sheet, press in place, remove the red plastic liner, and adhere. It is not repositionable.

Fusible web and double-sided tape

Interfacings

Interfacings are stabilizers that are incorporated into the construction of garments and accessories. They are like underwear. It's hidden, keeps things smooth and under control, and no one can see it.

Woven interfacings provide stability, is available in different weights, colors, and with a fusible treatment. They are usually made of cotton and may require pre shrinking. Non-woven interfacings are available with the same options as the woven but are synthetic.

Knit interfacings provide stretchable stability without distorting the drape, fusible convenience and are available in different colors. Most are made of nylon tricot and are available in a generous 60" width. A very lightweight version can be applied to Lycra knits, and a sheer version available in skin tones can be used with sheer fabrics.

Batting and Craft Fleece

The use of batting and craft fleece is usually interchangeable in the projects. Quilt batting is available in cotton and polyester. The cotton batting can shrink and result in a wonderful quilted look. Polyester batting will not shrink. Both types are soft and lightweight. When a stiffer or dense stability is needed in a project, use the craft fleece. Batting and craft fleece is also available as a fusible. This is a matter of personal preference. Test on a swatch, and record your findings in your journal.

Thread

This is such an exciting time to be a fiber artist because of all the thread that is available. Attend some sewing and quilting events, touch all the thread, and check to see how they look when sewn into fabric. Once again,

the local sewing machine dealership can help you with the selection. They offer classes to show how different threads produce different results with the various feet. The information on thread is diverse and there are many great books available.

Sewing Thread

There are a variety of sewing threads available for cotton fabrics, synthetics, silks, etc. Try different brands. Check for quality, color, price and availability. You don't want to run out of thread in a project that shows off the thread (such as an edge-stitched hem).

Decorative Sewing Thread

Now we're in the land of milk and honey. There is so much to choose from! These threads are available in every color, many weights (the larger the number, the finer the thread) and various fiber contents. You can find variegated (more than one color repeated on a spool), glow-in-the-dark, fusible, water-soluble, bright fluorescent, and low-lint threads, to name a few. Then there are metallic threads. Let me just say that you can't live without them. For the projects in this book I used polyester embroidery thread, rayon thread and fine metallic gold thread. Polyester thread adds a silken shine and strength, 30-wt. rayon thread is even more lustrous and fills the thread-painted area quickly, and the metallic thread just shows off.

Decorative Fibers

These fibers can be thick, chunky, and beautiful. Many of these threads cannot be threaded through the sewing machine. They can be hand wound onto a bobbin and used to work from the wrong side of the fabric. All of them can be "couched" (applied with another thread that holds them in place). Some are fusible for "no-sew" applications. The fusing agent is not visible and these can be applied with the heat of a mini iron and Teflon barrier.

Needles

For hand sewing, use a needle small enough to pass through the fabric with an eye large enough for the thread. Use a short needle (called betweens) specifically for quilting to stitch through layers easily. Sharps, a medium-sized needle, is used for general-purpose hand sewing. Needles are available in a variety of sizes, and the larger the number (#10 is fine), the smaller the needle.

Use the right sewing machine needles to make bigger projects go quickly. When there is a stitching problem, replace the needle as the first step of troubleshooting. It is important to select the right needle size for the fabric and thread for your project. Test the different needles with combinations of fabrics. Change the needle for every new project or every 8 to 10 hours of sewing.

Basic Parts

The shank is the heaviest part of the needle, and is the part that is inserted into the sewing machine. The shaft is the long, narrow portion, and the groove is on the front of the shaft to protect the thread as it moves through the fabric. The eye is the hole through which the needle passes. The point of the needle can be sharp or ball, and the scarf is on the back of the needle just above the eye.

Apply decorative threads with a mini iron.

Size 60 to 70 needle —	For sheer and lightweight fabrics
Size 80 to 90 needle —	For medium-weight to heavyweight fabrics
Size 100 to 120 needle —	For heavyweight upholstery fabrics
Leather needle —	Has a wedge-shaped point which allows it to penetrate leather and vinyl
Denim needle —	Has a sharp point and a very strong shank that allows it to go through layers of thick fabric
Embroidery machine needle —	Has a larger and longer eye to prevent thread from shredding and breaking
Ballpoint and stretch needles —	For knits; prevent stitches from skipping
Quilting needle —	Has a specially tapered point for sewing through multiple layers and intersections of fabric
Topstitch needle —	Has an extra-large eye and deeper groove in the shank for use with heavier fabrics and threads

Notions

Scissors, pins, pin cushion, tape measure, seam ripper and a seam gauge are the basics. The range of quality can be defined by price, so work within your means. Watch for sales and add to your supplies.

Rotary Cutter, Mat and Ruler

These items are essentials for cutting perfect strips and edges. The cutter has a rotating round blade attached to a handle. The cutting mat is made of a special healing plastic that doesn't dull the blade. The mat is marked with lines to use with a quilting ruler. The quilting ruler has lines in quarter-inch increments.

Marking Pens

Disappearing ink marking pens are great for use on light and medium-colored fabrics. The ink is usually blue and must be removed with moisture (on a paper towel, cloth or Q-tip) before pressing. A white marking pen is available for dark fabrics. The white color appears about ten seconds later. Chalk markers are available in a few light colors and are easily removed. Chalk marking spray is convenient for marking a large area and is easily removed by washing, the steam of an iron, or vacuum cleaner brush. Decorative marking pens are discussed in a later chapter.

Pressing Cloth

The pressing cloth is used as a barrier to protect the fabric. A 100% cotton cloth is ideal to use, especially when steam is required. Another option is the Teflon pressing sheet. This sheet is useful when working with fusible web. It will protect your iron as well as the project.

Other Tools

Fray stop spray stops the fraying of fabric and eliminates the need to finish edges. A chalk skirt marker marks hems accurately, quickly, and without assistance. A powder dispenser connected to a ruler leaves removable marks. You may also want to purchase a dress form. Select a dress form closest to your size with an adjustable feature. It is great for checking the fit and altered style.

Sewing Machine

The sewing machine manual and local dealership is the best source of information. You will want to become familiar with the different parts of your machine and how they work.

Feet

Most sewing machines now offer a variety of feet that expedite specific tasks. They're either packaged with the machine or can be purchased separately. For the projects in this book, it will be assumed that basic sewing will require the standard straight stitch foot and an appliqué foot (or similar) to switch to the zigzag stitch to finish edges and stabilize. Occasionally you will need the zipper foot. This foot is also useful to sew close to an obstruction (such as a magnetic snap). The darning or free-motion foot may have to be purchased separately. There are several models available. The basic model is the darning foot, a small metal circular frame that stays suspended above the throat plate even when the presser foot lever is down. It is used with the feed dogs in the "down" position. A free-motion foot may have a larger, clear frame with a spring which allows use with the feed dogs up.

Serger

The Serger (aka Overlocker) machine is another tool to achieve creative sewing, especially with knits. For the projects in this book, the serger is referred to as an option for finishing edges. Once again, the best place to see a demonstration is at a local sewing machine dealership.

Sewing Techniques

Seams

Seams are typically sewn with 12 stitches per inch. When a longer stitch length is needed to sew through a denser fabric or leather, a stitch length of 8 to 10 might be suitable. Test first on a swatch similar to the fabric you will be sewing. Test with different stitch lengths and needles.

A seam allowance may be ¼" (as in piecing for quilting), ½", or ⅝" (as in commercial patterns). Sometimes in a curved area, a smaller seam allowance may be used in combination with a stay-stitch line. When gathering, a deeper seam allowance is recommended. A fabric with a loose weave needs a deeper seam allowance (and possibly another row of stitching right next to the first) to prevent the seam from pulling apart. Experiment on swatches, and make notes in your journal.

After sewing a seam, it's best to press the seam, and then press it open. If the seam is not in a garment, and bulk is not an issue, you may just press it all to one side. Throughout the projects, be sure to press the seams open unless instructed otherwise.

Trim a seam to reduce bulk. A seam may be trimmed to a width of ¼" to ½", depending on the fabric and whether it is a stress area for the seam. If it is a sheer fabric, consider using pinking shears and trimming very little. For a fabric that frays, just trim the stray threads and finish the edge.

When pressing a seam, test your iron on a scrap first. When working with a combination of fabrics, use the setting suited to the most delicate fabric. Synthetics require a lower heat setting, even when teamed with a cotton.

Boxing the Corners of a Bag

This is a technique that creates width at the bottom of a bag — how wide is up to you. As you make the bag wider, the depth of the bag will shorten. You can pin or baste different widths before sewing to see if it appeals to you. If you need a purse with a firm bottom, measure the finished bottom and cut a square of plastic template material (slightly smaller); place it at the bottom of the purse. It can be placed between the purse and lining or covered with fabric and glued to the lining.

1 Fold the corner of the bag.

2 Measure from the point and make a horizontal line. Whatever the measurement is from the point to the horizontal line will result in double the amount for the width.

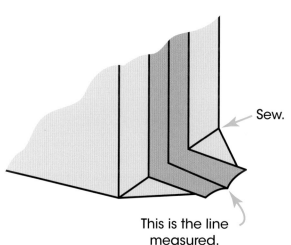

Sew.

This is the line measured.

Using Squares Creatively

Squares are a great way to frame objects to showcase and bring attention. The frame can also visually separate the item from another image. The color and width of your frame will do several things: it may make the square recede, jump forward, create the vignette, create a border or suggest importance.

Use the same technique as with the circles. Create squares and even triangles of any size and width. In place of the circle flounce at the sleeve, use a square. Use two squares, but layer them so there are eight points an equal distance apart. This will work with skirts, too. Squares can be created with the traditional log cabin piecing technique.

Using Circles Creatively

The circle is one of the most creative and useful shapes. The circle can be altered and used as patterns, design motifs, and layered to create concentric circles (one circle inside the other and sharing the same center).

A large circle can be used to create skirts. A wrap skirt can be created with two half circles. For a larger size, use three or four half circles. For a really dramatic effect, use two layers of sheer fabrics. A layer of sheer

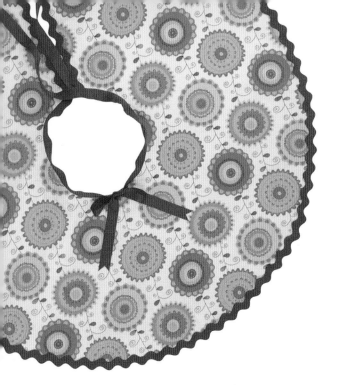

About a Circle

"Pi" allows you to find the circumference by multiplying the diameter by 3.14. Or you can work in reverse. With your waist measurement (circumference) divided by Pi, you can find the diameter and divide it in half for the radius. Use the radius to create and mark the inner circle which will be the waist area. Then, to add a seam allowance, just cut ½" above the circle.

Select a circumference (waist measurement) from the chart and use the corresponding radius. It is easy to fold the pattern paper into fourths, measure and mark the first radius. Add the skirt length to the first radius and mark a second circle on the pattern. Cut along both lines resulting in a full circle pattern. Add a seam allowance above the first line and a hem allowance below the second line. Use it as is or cut in half for placement on narrower fabric. Fold the fabric into fourths, pin in place, mark with a pen, and cut.

gray over a turquoise layer will create a muted shade of teal. Use it as a reversible skirt with the turquoise as the outer layer and the gray underneath. A sheer solid over a wild print will tone it down. When creating a closed skirt, the waist/inner circle must be able to slide over the hips to get to the waist. Using a knit fabric solves that problem because it will stretch with the waistband. If a woven fabric is used, the waist/inner circle must accommodate the hip measurement.

Use a medium circle for a short wrap skirt or an apron. An apron would be a great first project. It will allow you to see how different fabrics drape, how the waist/inner circle can dictate the fullness, and how to manage finishing the hem edge.

A small circle can add interest as a flounce on a sleeve edge and collar. Use a knit fabric that doesn't ravel to avoid having to finish the curved edge. If a finished edge is needed, fold the edge to the wrong side and edge stitch. Then, fold again and edge stitch once more. A rolled hem stitch with a serger would finish the edge in no time.

Use circles as a design motif. A group of circles creates the polka dot look. This allows you to select the background color, the color of the dots, and the dot placement. Large dots can be finished with an appliqué (satin stitch) edge. Smaller dots can be stitched near the edge and allowed to fray.

Tip:

The perimeter of a circle is called the circumference.

The radius is the measurement from the center point to any point of the circumference.

The diameter is the measurement across the circle passing through the center.

radius "	x 2 = diameter	x Pi = circumference
3	6	18.84
3.5	7	21.98
4	8	25.12
4.5	9	28.26
5	10	31.40
5.5	11	34.54
6	12	37.68
6.5	13	40.82
7	14	43.96
7.5	15	47.10
8	16	50.24
8.5	17	53.38
9	18	56.52
9.5	19	59.66

Making Circle Patterns

Use a protractor where you can. For longer distances, purchase a tape measure with a hole at the beginning. Place a pin through the hole and pin to the point of the folded paper. Lay the tape measure along the length of the paper and mark the lengths. The tape measure will be able to pivot from the point. Just remember that the hole in the tape measure is not placed at the very end. Measure the distance from the edge of the tape measure to the top of the hole. It will probably be a scant ¼". Add that to all your measurements. (String can work, too.)

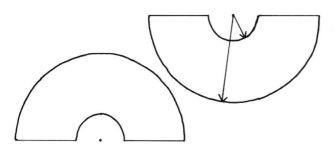

Tip:

Lightweight, sheer fabric like chiffon tends to wiggle during the layout and cutting. Do the best you can during the layout, and just cut. The hem will probably require some straightening out with the hem marker anyway. Don't stress on perfection. Remember, an uneven hem can be altered style!

Small Circle Patterns

1 Fold the paper into fourths.

2 Use a protractor or the method above to mark the inner and outer circles. After marking the inner circle, add a ¼" to ½" seam allowance to the inside of the circle and hem allowance if needed.

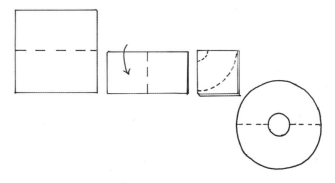

Closures

Grommets

Use large grommets on fabrics of substantial weight. When applying to a lightweight or medium-weight fabric, stabilize the area with iron-on interfacing. Smaller grommets are ideal for lightweight and medium-weight fabrics. A set of grommets has two parts. The side with prongs is called the washer, and the other side is called the eyelet. Mark the placement by tracing the inside opening of an eyelet. Cut out the hole. Insert the eyelet in the hole from the right side of the fabric. Place the washer over the eyelet with the prong side facing the eyelet. The application tool has two parts. The small, disc-like piece is the anvil which is placed under the eyelet. Place on a hard, protected surface. The second part of the application tool is the stud which is placed through the washer and into the barrel of the eyelet. Carefully and evenly, hammer the top of the tool.

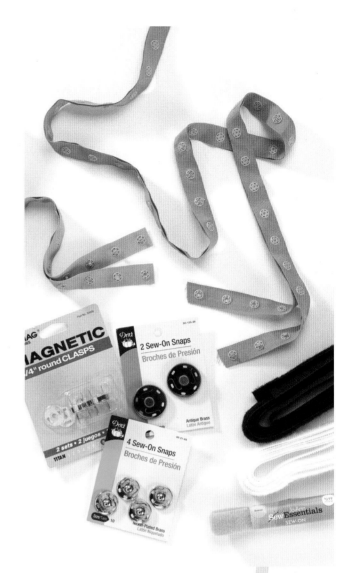

Eyelet Punches

The punch set is accompanied with changeable tips in various sizes. The tips cut perfect holes for belts and grommets. Mark the placement for the holes. Select the tip size and attach to the punch. Place the tip evenly vertical over the placement mark. Make sure a piece of wood is underneath the fabric or leather. Carefully and evenly, strike the top of the tool.

Heavy-Duty Snaps and Tool

This set of snaps has four parts. The decorative prong (which looks like the front of a button) will be applied to the socket (which has a small hole in the center). The stud has a protrusion in the center and will be applied to the plain prong (which is just a round frame with prongs). The application tool has two parts: the metal cup and the setter. Mark the placement for the snaps.

The decorative prong is pushed through the fabric. First, position the raised center of the socket over the prongs. Place the decorative side of the prong in the metal cup. Center the large end of the setter over the socket. Carefully and evenly, strike the top of the setter. The plain prong is pushed through the fabric. The stud is placed over the prongs with the protrusion facing away from the prongs. Place the ring side of the prong in the metal cup. Center the setter over the positioned stud and strike the top of the setter. Before starting, snap the socket and stud together. This will clarify how the other sides go into the prongs.

Magnetic Snaps

Mark the placement of the snaps with a dot. Place the center hole of the metal washer over the dot. Mark the two lines on the side of the dot. Use a seam ripper or sharp scissors to cut along those short lines. Place one side of the snap prongs through the slits. Place the washer over the prongs. If the snap is in a small area, fold the prongs toward the center. If not, fold the prongs away from the center. For more stability in a large area, add a larger washer (created from plastic template material) before the metal washer, and fold the prongs away from the center. Do the same for the other side of the snap.

Sew-on Snaps

The snap has two parts. One side has a small ball that protrudes, and the other side has a hole called the socket. The ball snaps into the socket. Mark the placement, unsnap the set and place the flat area of the back on the fabric. Using a threaded and knotted needle, send the needle through a few threads of fabric under the edge of the snap to hide the knot. Bring the needle up through the closest hole (around the perimeter of the snap). Send the thread over the snap rim and back down through the fabric. Depending on the stability and strength needed, repeat sewing through the hole two or three times. Send the needle under the snap to come through the next hole. Repeat the process and progress around the snap perimeter. To end, send the needle under the edge of the snap and tie a knot. Do the same for the other side of the snap.

Velcro

Velcro is a nylon two-part hook-and-loop tape to sew in. Keep the two pieces of tape paired, and cut the length as needed. Mark the placement. Pull the two sides apart. Sew each side in place along the edge of the tape. Velcro is available with an adhesive back for projects that will not be laundered. It is readily available in black, white and tan, and sometimes it is available in other colors and prints.

Embellishments

Bling

Hot-fix flat-back Swarovski crystals are available in many sizes, shapes and colors. They have a flat back, which is treated with an adhesive activated with heat. Marking the placement is optional. Once you start, you won't be able to stop. Place the fabric on a flat surface. An ironing board surface is ideal. Place the crystals on a Teflon sheet with the flat side down. Select a tip for the application tool that corresponds to the size of the crystal being used. Place the tip of the tool vertically over the crystal, and touch lightly. The crystal will be lifted by the tool. At first, look at the back of the crystal and you will see the glue puffing up. After a few crystals you will know how long it takes to heat the glue. Lightly place the back of the crystal down on the fabric. The crystal will adhere to the fabric. Continue with the next crystal.

Nailheads and Jewel Crystals

These items require the flat "hot spot" tip on the application tool. Place the items right side up on the fabric. Carefully, place the flat tipped tool on the nail head or jewel without moving. After setting a few pieces you will know how long it takes to heat the glue. These are my favorite embellishment.

Metal Studs with Prongs

Mark the placement. Push the prongs through from the right side of the fabric. Use an eraser to help push the prongs through the fabric. Press the prongs toward the center.

Acrylic Crystals

Acrylic crystals are available in a variety of shapes, sizes and colors, and there are various methods of application. These crystals are very inexpensive, and they are primarily used for crafting and applied with glue. Some have holes large enough through which to pass a needle for sewing. They are nowhere as brilliant as crystals, but they offer a fun way to incorporate big bling. Use acrylic crystals on garments that require infrequent washings.

Graffiti

Permanent Markers

These markers are versatile and can be used with paper, leather and fabric. They do not require heat to set. These pens are inexpensive and work well on most fabrics. They are ideal for projects and places where you are unable to set with heat. Test first on a scrap of fabric or an inside seam. If the fabric is lightweight or a loose weave, the ink may bleed. A light touch is essential in any case. A thick fabric with a brushed surface (such as denim) is a perfect surface that will have minimal bleeding.

Metallic Markers

Permanent markers are also available in metallic colors. They work in the same manner, but they may require just a few minutes to dry thoroughly. Test first on a scrap or inside seam.

Heat-set Markers

These pens require heat to set but offer a myriad of clear, wonderful colors. Some of them offer two different tips; usually, one is a fine point and the other is similar to a watercolor paint brush. You can do everything with these from detailed calligraphy to abstract brush strokes. A blender pen can be used to blend colors or a paint brush dampened with water can offer a watercolor technique. These pens offer all the creativity of paint in the convenience of a pen.

Dimensional Fabric Paint

These fabric paints are available in matte, slick, and metallic versions of almost every color of the rainbow. They can be squeezed out with a fine tip or brushed on to fabric with painterly strokes. When pearl colors are applied in dimensional dots, they dry resembling pearls. Crystals can be placed onto the paint while wet to set. Consider using the paints with stencils and rubber stamps for quick embellishment.

Iron-on Ribbon Thread

These beautiful metallic threads are $\frac{1}{16}$"- to $\frac{1}{8}$"-wide and available in many colors. You can find variegated and glow-in-the-dark version as well. They are treated with a fusible finish, which allows for quick and easy application. Pin the placement of the thread. To apply, use a mini iron wrapped with an adhesive Teflon sheet. Press with the iron for 15 to 30 seconds. Continue pressing in small sections, and cut away the remainder when finished. The heat sets it permanently.

Trims

Ribbons

Ribbons are available in every thickness imaginable and in even more colors and prints. Ribbons serve many purposes. They embellish (with bows), hold things together (like shoe lacings), and hide other techniques (such as thread and knots). Ribbons can be turned into straps for dresses and purses, and they can embellish while strengthening other straps. Use ribbon to lace through a series of slits to decorate a jacket, or send them through a row of grommets to change up a style. Write a message on a length of ribbon or your name to use as labels everywhere.

Feather Fringe

Feather fringe is available in a range of colors, lengths and types of feathers. The fringe consists of a tape that holds the feathers. Cover the tape with another embellishment, ribbon or strip of fabric. This is an easy and quick way to add elegance.

Dimensional Trims

Organza rose trim is sold by the yard and attached to a narrow elastic strip. This allows you to manipulate it in curves, group them in clusters, and place them on garments where a little stretch in imperative. It's available in half a dozen color schemes, but my favorites are the Victorian scarlet and black combination and the monochromatic green. The flowers are interspersed with a lofty rayon fiber. A petite rose trim set on satin ribbon is an option for a more demure embellishment also sold by the yard. A basic fiber trim can have a versatile effect, depending on the color. In a deep black it can look like an unusual fur, and a teal and peach trim can make you feel like you are on the bottom of the ocean.

Lace

Lace has been used for centuries, and it never goes out of style. Venetian lace usually has a distinct design that can be cut apart and joined easily, and you can even find it as a fringe. Lace can be purchased as yardage, in strips of every width, and as a motifs. It is readily available in bridal sections of fabric stores in the essential white and cream. Now it can be found in great colors of brown, black and turquoise. If you don't find what you want, dye it! If the lace is made of rayon, it will take the dye readily and retain that lovely sheen. Craft departments offer dyes for cotton, synthetics and silks that result in an even color. For a natural altered style, consider dipping in strong, hot tea.

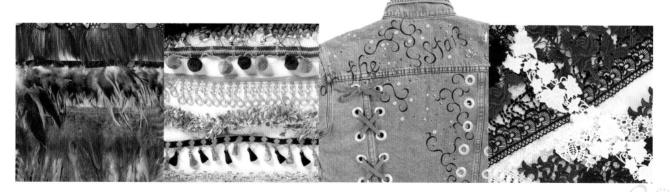

Something OLD

Cherishing something old is a way of honoring the past. It's extra special when handed down from a family member with memories of a time gone by. Vintage clothing has an air of romance and mystery, and it can transport you back in time. Many garments have proved that they can stand the test with timeless style. It may be difficult to find exactly what you want in the colors you desire, so create vintage style with contemporary fabrics. Take the time to add special details with buttons and trims. Most of all, take photos while having fun in these garments, write a little story, and hand it down.

Mom and Apple Pie Apron

This delightful apple-green reversible apron has a pocket on one side. The apron tie is yellow on both sides, and the pocket makes use of both fabrics. Three acrylic buttons add the finishing retro touch to the apron. I can just smell the apple pie!

Materials:

1½ yd. retro print fabric, 45" wide

1½ yd. of another retro print fabric, 45" wide

3 buttons

Matching thread

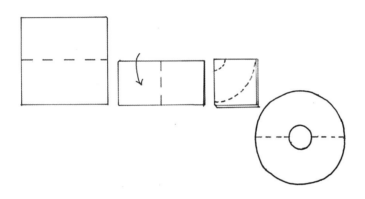

Instructions:

1 Create a half-circle pattern for the apron.

*The radius measurement from the center to the waist/inner circle is 7".

*The radius measurement from center to the hem/outer circle is 27".

Cut one apron from each of the two fabrics.

Cut a strip for the belt 5" wide and 36" long.

Create a circle pattern with a diameter of 7" for the pocket.

2 Pocket pattern

Open up the fabrics to a single layer and place them with RST. Place the straight edge of the circle sides parallel to the selvage edge of the fabrics. Place the tie pattern along the selvage, and cut two pieces out of the fabric selected for the ties. Place the pattern for the pocket on the remainder of the fabric. Pin and cut along the pattern lines (seam allowances are included).

Cut excess fabric from the corners.

3 Place the two apron fabrics with RST, sew the sides and curved hem of the apron with a ½" seam allowance. Clip the curved hem edge and cut the excess fabric from the corners. Turn right-side out and press.

Sew around the two circles, leaving an opening.

4 With the two pocket circles RST, sew around the perimeter with a ¼" seam allowance, but leave a 2" opening.

Clip around the circle curve. Turn right-side out through the opening. Tuck the seam allowance inside the opening and press. Topstitch one third of the pocket edge, which will become the "flap". Place the pocket to one side of the apron at a place convenient for your hand, and pin in place. Topstitch around the remainder of the circle pocket. For a reversible apron, use thread that matches each side of the apron.

Sew the buttons on the flap and pocket.

Sew the pocket to the apron.

5 Stay stitch along the top edge of the apron layers ½" from the edge. Clip the curve up to the stitch line.

6 Place the two long ties with RST. Sew one set of the short ends with a ¼" seam allowance. Fold the 5" width in half with RST. Sew the short ends with a ¼" seam allowance. Pin the long length of the tie along the raw edges.

7 Measure the top edge of the apron. Leave that measurement pinned and unsewn in the center of the tie. Sew the remaining sides of the tie with a ½" seam allowance. Turn the tie right-side out. Tuck the seam allowance inside the unsewn area and press.

8 Tuck the top of the apron inside the opening of the tie.

Bring the finished edge of the tie just below the stay-stitch line, and pin in place. Topstitch close to the edge around the entire tie, catching both sides of the opening.

Tuck the apron inside the tie.

The finished pocket.

Aunt Lulu Loves Pink!

Aunt Lulu never really cooked, but she always looked good in the kitchen. She said, "The way to a man's heart is through his stomach. If you can't do that, make sure you look better than the food." This cute, flirty apron is created with one layer of a medium-weight fabric and edged with jumbo pink rickrack and grosgrain ribbon.

To make this flirty apron, create a half circle pattern, following the directions for the Mom and Apple Pie Apron. Stay-stitch around the inner circle, and hem the bottom edge of your circle. Cover the bottom hem and raw edges of the apron with rickrack (about 3½ yards), and add a colorful ribbon to the waist. Looking good!

Dance The Polka Glasses Case

Polka dot is a pattern consisting of dots that can vary in size and arrangement. Polka dots became a popular design on clothing in the late 19th century at the same time polka music became popular. Adding a dot is a magical way to transform fabric in a chic instant. Use colors of a time gone by in a subtle print to re-create the past. Place them in an asymmetrical pattern, and watch them dance like notes on a music sheet.

Materials:

1 fat quarter each green, light blue and ecru fabric

1 fat quarter batting

Matching thread

Decorative threads

Disappearing ink pen

Fusible web with release paper

Heat-resistant Mylar template (optional)

Fabric glue

1 small set of snaps

Instructions:

1 Create a dot template with an inner and outer ring. Use the circle pattern provided. Cut along the inner circle.

2 Create a pattern for the eyeglass cases 6½" wide x 7½" long. Use the pattern to cut two of the fabrics and the batting. Place the two fabrics with RST and the batting underneath. Sew around the square with a ½" seam allowance, leaving a 3" opening to turn right-side out.

3 Trim the corners on the diagonal and the seam allowances to ¼". Turn right-side out. Tuck the seam inside the opening, pin, and press.

Stitch close to the edge around the perimeter.

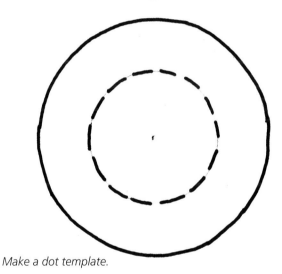

Make a dot template.

Sew around the rectangle.

Turn right-side out, and tuck the seam allowance inside the opening.

4   Place the dot template on the release paper of the fusible web. Trace the inner and outer circles. Cut along the outer circle. Trace and cut three small circles on the release paper using the inner circle.

Tip:

If it is difficult to trace through the fusible web and release paper, place them over a light table or hold the paper against a glass window.

5   Place the fusible side of the large circle and one of the small circles on the wrong side of the ecru fabric. Place a small circle on the wrong side of the green and blue fabrics. Press the fusible web according to the manufacturer's instructions. Cut all the fabrics along the outer edge of all the circles.

6   Fold the square in half with blue sides together and pin along the edge. Center the large ecru dot near the top (on the green side), with RST.

Pin the dot in place. Release the pin that kept the square folded in half so it lies flat.

Center the dot near the top.

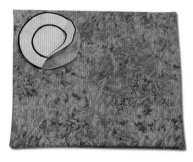

Pin the dot in place.

7   With the right side of the ecru circle placed on the green fabric, sew along the inner circle. Sew slowly, pivoting periodically with the needle in the down position, or use the free motion technique. Sew through the release paper, using it as a guide. Remove the release paper.

8 Trim away the space inside the inner circle, leaving a scant ¼" seam allowance. Clip around the circle curve.

9 Carefully, pull the ecru dot through the hole to the blue side. Pin the circle in place and press lightly. Sew close to the inside edge of the dot.

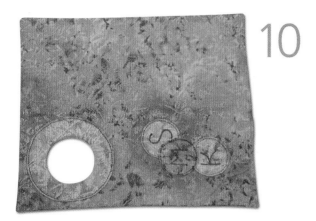

10

Stitch your initials on the circles.

10 Peel away the release paper and arrange the three small circles on the lower portion. Sew around the circles. Write your initials with the disappearing ink pen in the center of the circles. Use decorative thread to stitch the initials. Use a straight stitch or the free-motion stitch.

11

11 Apply a set of snaps in the top corners. This will allow you to snap it onto a purse handle strap.

Add snaps.

12 Fold the square in half, with the green sides together. Sew along the short bottom edge and the long side, leaving the top 2" unsewn.

Men Make Passes At Girls Who Wear Glasses

Cat-eye "peepers" studded with rhinestones worn with a bouffant beehive hairdo were "boss" on a "dolly" with a "classy chassis!" These glasses are back — but without the big hair! Eyeglass cases have become a major decorative accessory, no longer hidden in the deep recesses of your handbag. Everything is a-glitter with rhinestones, and if the "bling" isn't on the glasses, put it on the case.

Materials:

- 5" x 7" mauve suede
- 5" x 7" mint suede
- 6 hot-fix Fuchsia Swarovski crystals, 4 mm
- Mauve polyester thread
- Fusible decorative thread
- Mini iron with Teflon covering
- Heat-resistant Mylar template sheets
- Hot-fix crystal tool
- Pencil
- Permanent marker
- Quick-grab leather glue

Instructions:

1 Cut a 5"-wide x 7"-long rectangle out of the mauve suede.

2 Fold in half, and sew close to the edge of one short end and the long edge.

3 Use the eyeglass pattern provided, and trace onto the template material using a permanent marker. Cut the shape and one of the lens shapes.

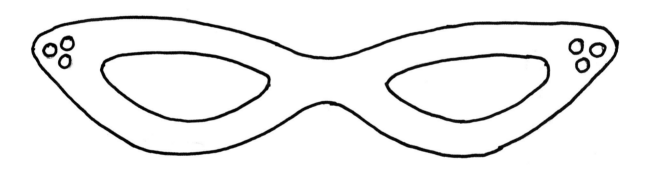

4 Place the template on the wrong side of the mint suede, and using a light touch with a pencil, trace the outline of the eyeglasses as well as the lens area. Flip the pattern over to trace the other lens area.

7

Front of the case.

Add iron-on bling to the back of the case.

5 Cut along the pencil lines with a sharp scissors. If you have special leather shears, they will spare your good fabric scissors.

6 Smear quick-grab leather glue on the wrong side of the suede cutout. Place them centered on the eyeglass case, and press in place.

7 Embellish the mint suede eyeglass cutout with three crystals in each corner, following manufacturer's instructions.

8 Place the fusible decorative thread around the eyeglass shape. Fuse in place with the Teflon-coated mini iron.

Coco Mocha Coin Purse

This morsel of a purse is fashioned after one of haute couture's favorite designers, Coco Chanel. She influenced fashion with her vision of expensive simplicity. Create your own designer accessories by splurging on small quantities of expensive materials. It takes very little metallic bronze leather and just a snippet of the faux leopard leather to create this sleek, chic porte-monnaie ("coin purse" in French).

Bakelite was invented by Leo Hendrik Baekeland in 1907. It was made from mixing carbolic acid and formaldehyde and is considered the first plastic. This new plastic transformed the world when it was used to make engine parts, insulation for electronics and jewelry. Bakelite jewelry and accessories became popular in the 1930's to 1940's, and pieces were offered by Coco Chanel.

This project allows you to create objets d'art in the Art Deco style with a readily available purse frame. The purse frame details are kept as authentic as possible. This design is based on the popular early 20th century Bakelite and celluloid frames.

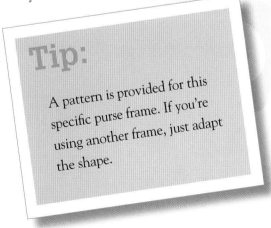

Tip:

A pattern is provided for this specific purse frame. If you're using another frame, just adapt the shape.

Materials:

Approx. 5" x 5" faux vintage purse frame

Metallic bronze leather

2" x 2" square faux leopard leather heart

6" x 6" lightweight material for frame facing

12 small beads (with holes large enough for the needle to pass through)

Polyester thread to match leather

Clear polyester thread

Beading needle

Double-sided adhesive tape

Leather sewing machine needle

Instructions:

1 Use Pattern #1 to cut two pieces of bronze leather for the body of the purse. Use Pattern #2 to cut two pieces of lightweight fabric and two pieces of double-sided adhesive tape. Use Pattern #3 to cut one piece of faux leopard leather and one piece of double-sided adhesive tape.

Cut the bronze leather, lightweight material and double-sided tape.

2 Place the two pieces of bronze leather with RST. Sew from the dot on one side to the dot on the other side as indicated. Backstitch to reinforce, when beginning and ending. Use a stitch length of 8 to 10 stitches per inch. Clip the curve with notches.

Notch the curve.

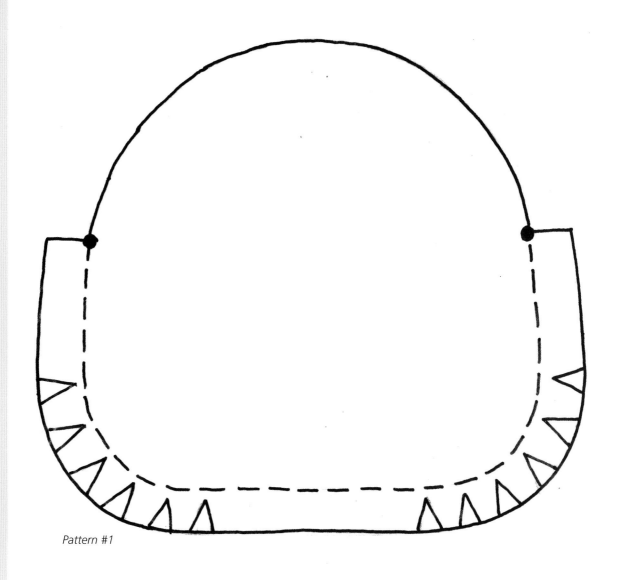

Pattern #1

Pattern #2

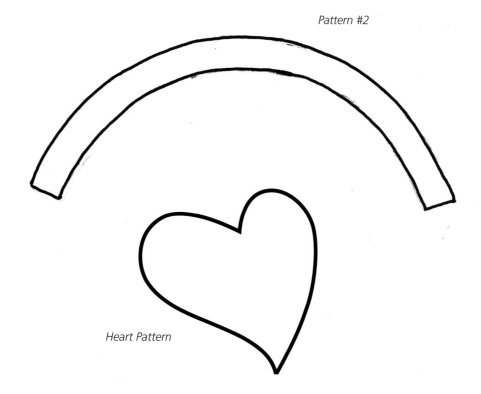

Heart Pattern

3 The purse frame has a channel. Slip the tops of the purse inside the channels on each side. Use pins as shown to hold it in the channel.

Thread the needle with a double length of thread. Create a large knot by knotting the end three times.

Hold the purse in the channel with pins.

4 Starting from the inside of the bag, send the needle through the hole at one end of the frame. Add a bead and go back through the hole to the inside.

Send the needle through the next hole, and repeat until all the holes have a bead.

Send the needle through the hole.

5 After the last bead, slip the needle under the thread that is coming from the previous hole, and tie a knot.

Tie again two more times to secure. Cut the threads. Repeat steps 3-5 for the other side of the frame.

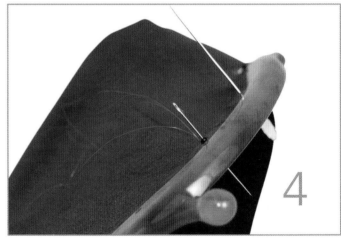

Repeat until all holes have beads.

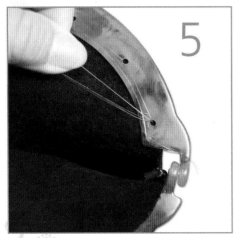

Tie a knot.

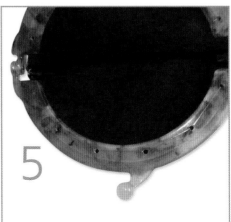

Repeat for the other side of the frame.

6

Place tape on the lightwight fabric.

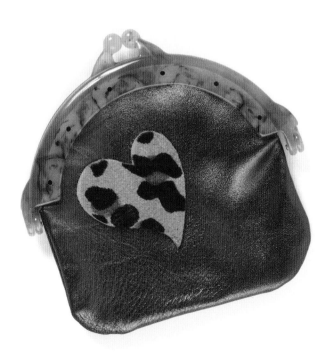

6

Press tape to the inside of the purse frame.

6 Peel one of the layers of plastic off the double-sided adhesive tape. Place and press it on the lightweight fabric of the same shape.

Peel the last layer of plastic off the tape, and press it in place on the inside of the purse frame to cover and protect the threads.

7 Repeat step 6 for the other side.

8 Prepare the leopard heart in the same manner as in step 6. Press in place on the purse.

Ginza Fashionista Purse

The Ginza is a district of Tokyo located south of Kyobashi, west of Tsukiji, east of Uchisaiwaicho and north of Shinbashi. It is a fashionista's paradise, with many department stores, boutiques and restaurants. This beautiful piece of handpainted silk may have been worn by a woman of style who shopped there regularly.

The silk came from the lining of a vintage Haori, a short kimono-style jacket that is worn over a full-length kimono. Many women in Japan have given up wearing the traditional clothing, and it is being taken apart and refashioned as purses, quilts and contemporary fashion. The vintage silk and metal purse frame with rhinestones are a perfect match.

Materials

- 2 pieces vintage silk, 8½" x 11"
- 2 pieces lining, 8½" x 11"
- 11" x 16" batting
- 11" x 16" medium-weight woven fusible stabilizer
- Metal purse frame with rhinestone handle
- Small beads (larger than the holes in the purse frame)
- Fine hand sewing needle (small enough to fit through the bead holes)
- Matching thread
- Clear polyester thread or beading thread

Tips:

The fabric requirements are given in exact measurements because vintage Kimono fabric is no wider than approximately 12", and many times the design runs only in one direction. Cut each piece separately, placing the rectangle in the landscape position (using the 11" dimension as the width).

The edges of the holes on the purse frame can cut through regular thread, so consider using strong beading thread. Make sure you have a needle that can be threaded and still fit through the holes. For this project, I added small beads along the outside of the frame. These beads hold the thread away from the holes in the frame. Once the purse is attached to the frame, the stitching can be seen from the inside of the purse. Consider covering the stitching with a narrow ribbon that can be attached with glue.

Consider adding beads or a little hand embroidery. This is a great opportunity for altered creativity!

Tip:

This pattern was created for this purse frame. The finished bag is tucked into the crevice of the frame and sewn in. Frames without holes are attached with a crimping tool.

Instructions:

1 Place the two vintage silk pieces with RST. If the print is directional, place them facing upright. Pin the "bottom" 11" edge, and sew with a ½" seam allowance. Press the seam open.

2 Fuse the stabilizer to the batting, and place the wrong side of the silk on the other side of the batting. Pin in several places.

3 Use free-motion stitching to quilt through the layers. Use large sweeping, curved lines to avoid shrinking the fabric. Set up the sewing machine for free motion, and use decorative threads. (Or use the straight stitch and sew rows of lines.)

4 Fold in half with RST so that the width is still 11". Pin and sew the sides with a scant ½" seam allowance. Make sure that the opening at the top is still 21". Trim the seams. Do the same for the lining.

Place the purse and lining RST.

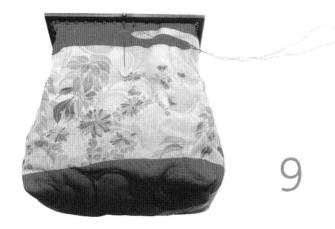

Send the needle out of the holes in the frame.

Back of the purse.

5 Measure 1½" from the corner, and box the corners. This will create a 3"-wide side. Do the same for the lining. Refer to page 15 for more information about boxing the corners.

6 Place the purse and lining with RST. Sew around the top with a ½" seam, leaving a 4" opening. Turn right-side out through the opening. Tuck the seam allowance inside the opening. Hand-stitch the opening closed.

7 Mark the center of the front and back with a pin.

8 Center the front of the purse with the center of the frame. Insert the opening of the bag in the narrow slot in the frame. Sew from the center to the side, and then from the center to the other side. Keep checking the fit as you sew. You may have to "ease" to fit. Do the same for the back.

9 Attach the purse to the frame by using a needle threaded with a double length of clear polyester thread with a large knot. As explained in step 8, start in the center inside of the bag, and send the needle out of the holes in the frame.

String a bead, and send it back through the same hole. From the inside, send the needle to the next hole, or skip a few holes. Periodically, when the needle is sent back to the inside, tie a knot to secure. The beads not only embellish the purse, but they keep the thread away from the edge of the metal holes. The knots add stability. When finished, glue a narrow ribbon over the stitching.

Caesar's Palace

Start with a small base of stabilizer about 3" wide x 1½" long with rounded corners. Use glue to cover the stabilizer with fabric, and add a pin to the back.

Add feathers, and curve to fit the width of the bag. Cover the trim that holds the feathers with more feathers. Add crystal beads to a stone doughnut with wire wrapping. Crimp the wire with a pair of needle-nose pliers to create an angular design as well as to "tighten" the wire around the stone.

To make this charming purse, add feathers with glue, and bend in a curve to fit the width of the bag. Cover the trim that holds the feathers with more feathers. Add a frog rhinestone pin.

Black Tie
at the CMAs

Use a child's denim overalls to create this bag. Carefully place the pattern over parts that you wish to use. Center the pattern on the bib area to incorporate the pocket. If the bib is smaller than the pattern, add fabric to the bib.

Use rayon braid cording to meander over the denim fabric. Sew in place by hand, machine stitch, or use glue to adhere. Add a strip of beaded fringe on the underside of the bib pocket flap. If the bib doesn't have a flap, create one with the extra fabric. Don't forget to decorate the back of the purse by adding black rayon tassels to match.

Back of the purse.

Magnolia Blossoms Jacket

The great part about having an old white twill jacket that is turning a pale yellow is that it can be bleached back to a pure white. Over the years, it seems that this jacket shrank while sitting in the closet. Funny how that happens! Now, it was too beautiful to part with and it had special memories. In its day it went to concerts, strolled art festivals, and even matched a pair of jeans. The juxtaposition of embellishing thick, cotton fabric with a delicately patterned lace to transform a sporty garment into one of elegant shabby chic was the answer.

Tip:

It is difficult to say how much lace is needed. Take the jacket to audition the laces and get the exact amount needed. Use laces of different widths. Select lace slightly wider than the collar, cuff and waistband. The portion that extends past the fabric will show, and the design will be appreciated. Select a wide, stunning lace for the back.

Materials:

White denim or twill jacket

Lace in varying widths

White thread

Clear polyester thread

Denim needle

Free-motion foot

Fray check

Instructions:

1. Thread the machine with clear polyester thread, and fill the bobbin with white sewing thread.

2. Place the straight edge of the lace along the inside edge of the collar. Pin in place. Sew the straight edge with a zigzag stitch to anchor. Then use the darning foot and free-motion technique over the lace to keep in place. Anchor the lace with rows of stitching. Anchor the lace around the perimeter edge of the collar.

3. Repeat step 2 the same for the cuff and waistband. Adding the lace at the waistband will make the jacket appear longer.

Begin with a white denim jacket.

Anchor the lace around the edge of the collar.

First layer of lace.

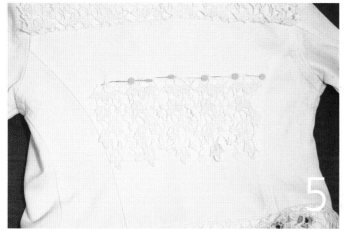

Second row of lace.

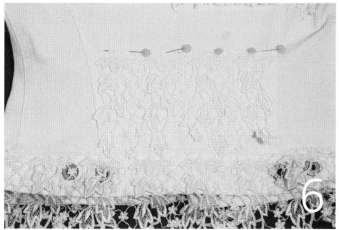

Last row of lace and row along the bottom edge of the jacket.

4 The back of the twill jacket usually has a center panel framed with flat felled stitching. Place the wide lace across the top of the back center panel. Cut to fit. Don't forget to treat the lace with fray check and let dry where it will be cut.

5 Place another portion of the lace slightly under the top row.

Cut to fit aligning the bottom of the lace to the width of the center panel.

6 Repeat step 5 until the center panel is covered.

Tip:

Consider adding clear Swarovski crystals and pearl beads, and weaving narrow satin ribbon through the lace design.

Back of the jacket.

Something NEW

Try adding something new to your wardrobe by just creating and altering circles and squares. It's convenient and inexpensive. You know how to draw a circle, so you don't have to go out and purchase anything, and you're ready to start. Surely, you have fabric waiting to be transformed!

Squares can turn into eyeglass cases, backpacks and purses. Circles can be used to create skirts, gowns and flounces for collars and cuffs. The possibilities are endless!

Safari Backpack

The Safari Backpack is just what a world traveler needs. Whether it's a short trip for a mocha latte, biscotti and a copy of "The Devil Wears Prada," or a trip to see the pyramids, the great motifs and earthy colors of the tapestry teamed with the mock crocodile will set you off on your journey in style.

Materials:

½ yd. safari tapestry fabric, 45" width

½ yd. green lining fabric, 45" width

2 sheets of black mock croc, 8½" x 11½"

1 sheet of green mock croc, 8½" x 11½"

2 pieces fusible web with release paper,
   15" wide x 13" long

2 adjustable purse handles with silver hardware

2 silver swivel clasps

1 package of alphabet brads

Decorative pin (optional)

Decorative rings, chain, and hook (optional)

Masking tape and pen

Seam ripper

5" strip of 1" double-sided tape

Thread to match the lining fabric

Clear polyester thread (or match croc colors)

Leather or denim sewing machine needle

Pressing sheet

Instructions:

Prepare the Fabrics

1 Cut two pieces of tapestry fabric, two of the lining, and two of fusible web 15" wide x 13" long.

2 Cut two 15" wide x 3" long strips of tapestry fabric to finish the opening.

3 From the black mock croc, cut one 10½" x 6" piece for the bottom, one 8"-wide x 2½"-long piece for the pocket flap and four 1"-wide x 3"-long pieces for handle tabs, and two 1"-wide x 3"-long pieces for closure tabs attached to swivel clasps.

From the green mock croc, cut one 8"-wide x 6½"-long piece for the bottom of the pocket, one 5"-wide x 1"-long piece to cover the brad prongs inside the pocket, and one 2"-wide x 5½"-long piece for the small handle.

4 Press the fusible web on to the wrong side of the lining fabric. For the pressing time, check the manufacturer's instructions. Use the Teflon sheet as a pressing cloth to protect the iron from accidentally touching some of the fusible web. Let cool and remove the fusible web release paper.

5 Place the wrong side of the lining/fusible web to the wrong side of the tapestry and press. Use the pressing sheet.

Outside Pocket

1 Consider adding a message to your backpack pocket. I used metal brads knowing I would not be throwing it in the washer. If you need a more durable pack, consider embroidering the words with thread. The word JOURNEY has seven letters, and the R will be in the center.

2 Measure 2½" from the top of the green mock croc pocket edge. Place the top edge of the masking tape on that line.

Place a dot on the center of the tape. Center a brad over the dot and mark the width on the tape. Move the brad over to the left, leaving a small space, and mark the next brad. Repeat marking three brad spaces to the left and three to the right of the center brad.

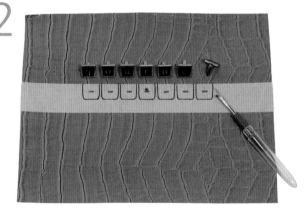

Mark brad spaces to the left and right of the center brad.

3 Measure ¼" down from the top of the tape and make a horizontal mark in the center of each brad space. Use a seam ripper to cut a slit just large enough to squeeze the brad prongs through. Remove the masking tape. Place the brad prongs through the slits. Open and finger press the brad prongs flat on the wrong side of the mock croc.

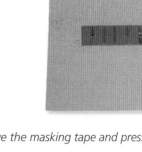

Remove the masking tape and press the brad prongs flat.

4 Place the double-stick tape strip over the prongs by first peeling away the protective plastic. Finger press in place, and then remove the second piece of plastic from the double-sided tape.

Cover the clear sticky area with the green mock croc strip. Finger press in place.

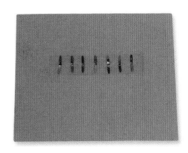

Remove the second layer of tape.

5 Cut four ¼" pieces of tape, and place a piece on each corner of the wrong side of the pocket. Place the pocket on the center of one of the tapestry pieces (which serves as the front). Place the bottom of the pocket 2" from the bottom edge of the tapestry. Remove the tape covering, and finger press the pocket into place. This eliminates the need for pins.

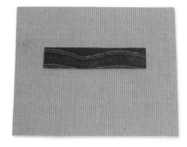

Cover the sticky area with mock croc.

6 Thread the machine with clear polyester thread or thread that matches the croc colors. Fill the bobbin with clear thread or thread that matches the lining. Set the stitch length to 8 to 10 stitches per inch. Stitch close to the edge of the sides and bottom of the pocket. Make sure to backstitch to secure when beginning and ending. Stitch again about ⅜" from the edge of the pocket, parallel to the first row of stitching. The two lines of stitching will offer a sporty look while adding stability.

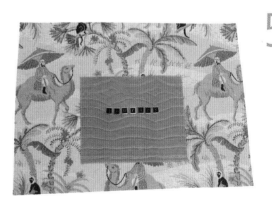

Finger press the pocket in place

7 Place two small pieces of tape on the wrong side of the top of the pocket flap. Place the top edge of the flap 1½" from the top edge of the pocket, or adjust as necessary for visual appeal.

Align the sides with the sides of the pocket. Remove the tape covering, and finger press into place.

8 Stitch across the top edge of the flap. Stitch again about ⅜" from the edge of the flap.

Adjustable Handles

1 Each adjustable handle has a ring on each end. Place a tab through each ring with the right side of the mock croc facing out. Bring the short ends together, and stitch close to the edge to hold in place.

2 Pin the adjustable handle tabs 5" apart, centered at the bottom of the second piece of tapestry (which serves as the back). Sew in place with a ⅜" seam allowance, and backstitch to secure.

Clasp Closure

1 Place one of the 1½" black mock croc tabs through each swivel clasp ring. Fold the tab with the right side of the mock croc facing out, and bring the two short ends together and stitch close to the edge. Do the same for the other strip. Use the same method as for the adjustable strap tabs.

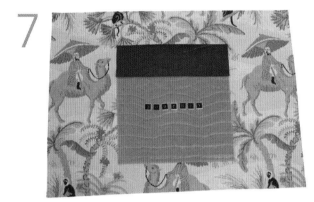

Place the flap on the pocket.

Sew the handles in place.

Small, Green Handle

1 Fold the green mock croc strip in half to a 1" width. Sew close to the long edge. Sew again ⅜" from the edge. Use the same threads in the machine and bobbin to match the front pocket.

Sew the small, green handle.

Assemble the Backpack

1 Mark the center of the bottom of each tapestry piece with a pin. Match it with the center of each long 8½" side of the black mock croc bottom piece. Place them with right sides together, and pin in place (or use clips).

Sew each pinned length with a ½" seam allowance, BUT begin and end ½" from the edge of the mock croc length. Backstitch to secure when beginning and ending.

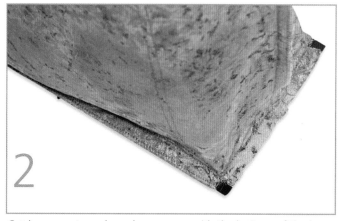

Pin and sew tapestry to black mock croc bottom piece.

2 Continue sewing with the clear polyester thread, or change the threads in the machine and bobbin to match the lining fabric. Place the two tapestry/lining pieces with tapestry sides together and sew the side seams with a ½" seam allowance. Trim the seams. Use a wide zigzag stitch to finish the edges.

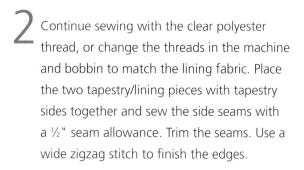

Cut in corner to make a sharp corner with the bottom of the bag.

3 Make a small cut in the tapestry fabric where the previous stitching started and stopped.

Align the remaining two sides of the tapestry with the two remaining edges of the black mock croc bottom. Pin and sew in place with a ½" seam allowance. Trim away any uneven edges or threads. Use a wide zigzag stitch to finish the edges. Turn the backpack right-side out.

Turn the backpack right-side out.

4 Center the tabs (with the swivel clasps) over each side seam on the inside lining. Align at the top. Pin and sew in place with a ⅜" seam allowance, and backstitch to secure.

Sew the tabs with swivel clasps to the inside lining.

5 The remaining two tapestry strips will create a binding to finish the top of the backpack. Place the two long tapestry strips with RST. Stitch the short ends with a ½" seam allowance. Press the seams open. Use a zigzag stitch to finish the edges. Use the zigzag stitch to finish the raw edges on both sides.

Mark the tapestry strip with pins.

6 Place the tapestry strip around the top of the backpack with RST. Line up the side seams. Align the edges at the top, and pin all the way around.

7 The small, green handle closure will be placed at the center front. Measure 3" in the center front, and place pins on the tapestry strip to mark.

The pins to the right show where the other end of the green strip will go later. The finishing band is sewn, leaving these two openings because the back adjustable straps have to be captured by the small green handle, and then the handle ends are sewn into those two opening.

Sew all the way around the top with a ½" seam allowance, except where the 3" space is marked. Trim the seam allowances of everything except the binding strip.

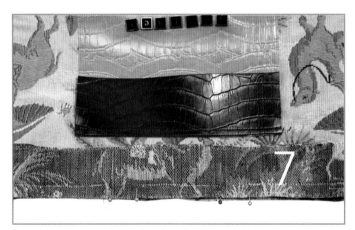

Mark the tapestry strip with pins.

8 Press the binding strip up. Place the binding strip over the seam allowances and bring the zigzag finished edge past the previous seam on the inside of the backpack. Pin in place. Sew close to the binding edge with a straight stitch all the way around, except for those two 1" spaces.

9 Place one of the ends of the small green handle into the 1" space. Make sure to push it ½" into the space. Pin in place. Sew close to the edge of the binding over the small green handle. This small green handle will have the stress of the weight of the backpack. You may want to reinforce it with an extra row of stitching.

10 Place the two adjustable handles in front of the green handle. Tuck the other end of the small green handle into the other 1" space. Pin and sew in place close to the binding edge.

Finish the binding.

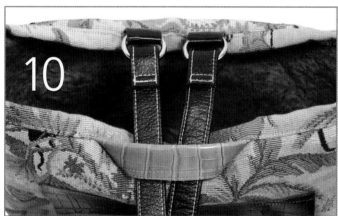

Pin and sew handles in place.

11

Add a decorative pin.

11 Add a decorative purchased pin or some matching hardware to make finding your keys a little easier.

Front of the pack.

Back of the pack.

Breakfast at Tiffany's Wrap Skirt

The versatile wrap skirt is a must have in your wardrobe. The convenience of style and simplicity of design, not to mention expandable size, make this a great novice project.

This wrap skirt is gathered for even more fullness. It is lined with another layer of fabric which darkens the green turquoise background and defines the elegant black roses. The fabric measurements are just an approximation because the actual amount will be determined by your measurements and skirt length. The fabric has a 60" width, which allows for a long length. The inner circle (for the waist) is larger than usual because some of it will be gathered and some of it will be crossed over during the wrapping. The amount of overlap is up to you, but be sure there is enough. In this case, a 6" overlap is used for a 30" waist.

Materials

- Chiffon fabric (see step 1 for yardage)
- Lightweight polyester black fabric
  (see step 1 for yardage)
- Sewing thread to match
- Pattern paper, string and pencil

Instructions:

Pattern and Layout

1 Create a half-circle pattern. Three half circles will be needed.
Waist measurement = A, (30")
A divided by Pi (3.14) = B, the diameter (10.5")
B divided by 2 = C.
C is the radius for the inner circle (5.25")
D is the radius for the outer circle (33") inner circle radius plus the length of the skirt (includes a 1" hem allowance) =
(5.25 + 27.75) or 33"

2 Create a pattern for the waistband tie. The finished width is 2". Double it, and add 1" for seam allowances = 5" width. The length depends on the waist measurement (30" x 2 for the "wrap" = 60"), size of the bow, and the length of the bow tails (another 60" = 120"). Use a long ribbon to wrap around the waist twice, tie into a bow with tails to drape to determine the length needed for the tie. Cut these ties along the cross grain or grain of the black fabric. Since two strips will have to be joined to create this extra long strip, cut two strips 5" x 60".

Assemble the Skirt

3 Cut three half circles out of the chiffon fabric. Place two pieces with RST, pin, and sew the straight side seams. Finish the edges with a second line of stitching and use pinking shears to finish the edge or serge the edges. Select one of the two joined pieces to become the center and repeat the process by adding the third skirt piece. Do the same with the black fabric.

4 Finish the two side seams by folding the edge to the wrong side ¼" and stitching close to the edge. Then fold again to the wrong side and stitch close to the edge (or serge the edges).

5 Place the two layers of skirts with WST and pin along the inner circle. If one of the fabrics stretches more than the other, ease to match them up.

6 To gather the waist, use a slightly longer stitch length (8 to 10 stitches per inch), and stitch ¼" from the fabric edge. Begin and end with long thread tails. Then stitch a second row ¼" from the first.

7 To determine how much to gather: The waist measurement (30") plus the overlap (12") equals 42". Gather the waist area to that measurement. Do not gather the last 6" at both ends where the skirt will overlap. Fabrics with a tight weave will appear to have fewer gathers and a loose weave will result in more gathers. For a very full skirt, add a fourth skirt half circle and eliminate the lining and wear with leggings.

8 Pull two of the thread tails from one end of the skirt. The two you select will be on the right side of the fabric. Pull evenly and carefully. Move the gathers evenly toward the center. Do the same from the other end. Do not place gathers at the overlapping ends. Place a pin and wrap the thread tails around the pin to hold in place.

9 Create the strip length needed for the waistband tie by placing the strips with RST and sewing one of the short ends with a ½" seam allowance and press the seam open. Place the center of the tie at the center of the gathered area of the skirt. Pin the length of the gathered area to the tie with RST. Sew the length of the gathered area to the tie using the lower row of stitching as a guide (½" from the edge of the fabric). Trim to ¼".

10 Fold the tie width in half with RST. Pin the short ends and then the length of the tie up to the gathered area. Sew with a ½" seam allowance. Trim the seam allowance to ¼" (unless it is a loose weave with a tendency to fray). Turn right-side out and press.

11 Tuck the remaining seam allowance (along the gathered length) under and pin in place just below the lowest gathering stitch.

12 Stitch around the entire perimeter of the tie, making sure to catch the opening on the back of the tie.

13 Put the skirt on (or use a dress form) and use a chalk marking tool to mark an even hemline all the way around. Cut through the chiffon and black lining. Let it hang overnight. Sometimes, it will stretch a bit more. Repeat with the chalk tool.

14 Finish the edge of the chiffon layer by straight stitching in the same manner as the sides.

15 Trim the black fabric an inch shorter and finish the edge in the same manner.

French Riviera Sweater

Alter a sweater to match the skirt. Use a narrow braid cording and weave it through the sweater. Hand sew the beginning and ending to the inside of the sweater. This also helps stabilize a sweater that has stretched.

Begin with a plain sweater.

Thread a large upholstery needle with braid cording.

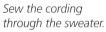

Sew the cording through the sweater.

Pretty In Pink
Blouse

If you've seen *Pretty in Pink*, you know that the protagonist uses her sewing and fashion skills to create her unique altered style, New-Wave clothing.

Can't find what you want? Design it and make it! Use an easy blouse pattern with a soft, lightweight knit. Knit fabric is very forgiving while offering a great drape—and the best part is the ease of fit. The "raw edges" on this top are part of the cutting edge style.

Tip:

Use an easy blouse pattern with a Dolman sleeve. The sleeve part of the pattern is attached to the body of the blouse. This eliminates the need for set-in sleeves. It is also a comfortable style for knits. The shoulder/ upper arm area is loose and tapers to a more fitted sleeve. Select a pattern with a V-neck shape to add an altered flounce.

Create the patterns for the flounce collar and cuff to get accurate measurements for fabric requirements.

Materials

Blouse pattern with a "V" neck (or a
   purchased top)

Floral knit fabric for the top (see pattern for
   yardage)

1 yd. pink knit fabric for the collar and
   sleeve edge

Sewing thread

Ballpoint needle

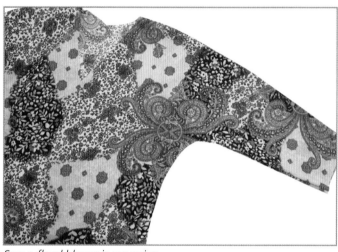

Sew a floral blouse in your size.

Instructions:

Prepare the Blouse

1 Use the purchased pattern and cut the front
and back in your size. Use the accompanying
instructions for the layout information
and seam allowance. Consider using a
narrow, longer-length zigzag stitch for the
construction.

2 Sew a line of stay stitching along the seam
allowance. If there is no seam allowance
lines on your purchased pattern, read the
accompanying instructions. If the seam
allowance is ⅝", sew the stay-stitch line ⅝"
from the edge.

3 Trim the seam allowance to ¼".

4 Decide on a good sleeve length. The flounce
will add about 4". Shorten the sleeve length
by 3¾". An extra ¼" is left on the sleeve to
allow for the seam allowance.

Tip:

One circle would create a very
subtle flounce for the collar.
Using the two circles will create
a flounce with more folds. One
circle is used for the sleeve.

Mark the inner and outer circle.

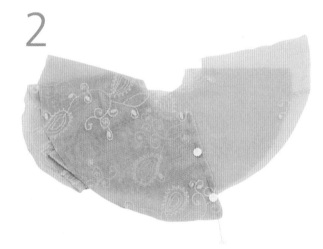

Place cut edges together to create a larger circle.

Create Patterns for the Collar and Sleeve Flounce

1 Measure the V-neck opening, and divide that measurement in half because two circles will be used to create the collar.

The measurement of the neck opening divided by 2 = V.

V divided by two = W, the circumference of the inner circle of the flounce.

W divided by 3.14 = X, the diameter.

X divided by two = Y, the radius for the inner circle of the flounce.

The width of the collar is 4". Y plus the collar width (4") = Z, the radius of the outer circle.

2 Fold the paper into fourths. Mark the radius of the inner circle. Mark the ¼" seam allowance above the inner circle. Mark the outer circle.

Cut along the seam allowance inner circle and along the outer circle. Make a cut along one of the folds from the inner circle to the outer circle.

3 Do the same for the sleeve flounce, using the sleeve edge measurement for "W".

Assemble the Collar and Sleeve Flounce

1 Cut two collar circles and two sleeve circles out of the knit fabric.

2 For the collar, place one of the cut edges from each circle with RST. Do the same with the remaining two cut edges, creating a larger circle.

Finish the collar.

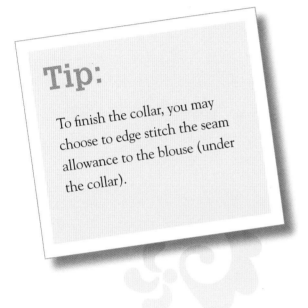

Tip:

To finish the collar, you may choose to edge stitch the seam allowance to the blouse (under the collar).

3 Place the right side of the collar on the neckline on the wrong side of the blouse. Place one of the seams at the center back of the blouse and the other seam at the center front. Ease and pin the collar to the neckline. Sew with a ¼" seam allowance. Clip through the seam allowance around the curve of the back of the neck and at the "V" point in the front. Clip up to but not through the seam.

4 Flip the collar over to the right side of the blouse. Press the neckline edge.

5 To add the flounce to the sleeve, divide the inner circle in half and mark with pins. Divide the sleeve opening in half and mark with pins. Place the flounce and sleeve edge with RST. Match the pins on the sleeve edge and inner circle. Pin and ease the rest of the circle around the sleeve edge. Sew with a ¼" seam allowance.

5

Deco Deity Tee

The sophisticated color combination, reminiscent of the Art Deco era, was the inspiration for this stunning tee. It was a time of sleek lines, luxuriously draped fabric and bold design. The simple yet striking curved lines of the rose echo the fabric used for the sleeve flounce.

Purchase a T-shirt and add rose motifs, Swarovski crystals and flounce sleeves. Use fabric paint, disappearing ink pen, freezer paper and a small tracing table to transfer and create the rose image. Transform a little leftover fabric from a skirt into a sleeve flounce.

Select an image from the fabric to replicate with altered style. In this case, there were black roses. Use a few curved lines to create roses and leaves or use the one provided. Transfer the lines with a black marker on to a sheet of paper. Place the image under the T-shirt and tape it in place. Place the small tracing table under the paper. Use the disappearing ink pen to transfer the lines on to the T-shirt. Place a sheet of freezer paper under the area to be painted. Be sure to place the slick, moisture repellent side of the paper up. Pin in place.

Use a black matte dimensional fabric paint in a squeezable dispenser with a fine tip. Practice on some fabric to gain control. Practice starting and stopping. Press on the fabric while squeezing a constant amount of paint while following the lines. Start with the images farthest away from where your hand is positioned. Pay attention as you are squeezing the paint because sometimes there is an air bubble "burp" which can compromise your steady line. Let it all dry overnight and the thickness of the lines will shrink a little.

Embellish with paint and crystals.

Mermaid Sea Queens Tee

The thing about bling is the more you have, the more you want. Remember that top with the very subtle opalescent sequins? You thought it was high flash, but now it's lost its dash. Add some vertical wiggly lines of AB hot-fix crystals in between the existing sequins, and the glimmer from the Aqua AB crystals will give the look of an underwater scene. Start with a line in the center, and work your way out. Add a line to the left a few inches away, and do the same to the right. Repeat until you are pleased. If that's not enough, place a few crystals in between the vertical lines.

A little girl who lives next door to me loves anything that sparkles. She saw the original T-shirt and asked what was sparkling. I explained that it was "sequins," disk-shaped beads made of plastic. So when she saw the altered tee with the Aqua AB crystals, she exclaimed, "Oh, I love the Mermaid Sea Queens!"

Tip:

To create this look with a plain T-shirt, use the instructions above and add your own sequins. For a quick fix, use Transmission AB crystals; they give off an opalescent shimmer while showing the color of the fabric underneath. Clear Diamond crystals offer a more traditional bling. Use 10ss (3 mm) crystals for a subtle sparkle, and use 20ss (5 mm) crystals to shine across the room!

Something BORROWED

You don't always have to buy something new and end up with the same fashion fad that everyone else has. You loved everything in your closet at one time and you still love it, so just freshen it up. Add the latest bling of choice. Instead of wearing the Swarovski earrings, place the sparkle on your purse, scarf, swim suit, and everywhere you want to shine. For an organic look add antique brass grommets and a heavy-duty metal zipper. Use some chains, charms and a swivel snap hook as a zipper pull. Everything does double duty as a working embellishment. So, go to the closet (not just yours — raid your friends' wardrobes for other ideas) and see what you can make over. Challenge yourself! The criteria can be: how quickly and easily it was accomplished, how little you spent by using something from your supplies, or how sublime the design is (really, someone should send you to Paris!)

Before you pack your bags for France, start with some simple projects for immediate gratification. Go shopping where it is free, you can show up in your pajamas, and everything is in your size — your closet.

Hermes Messenger Bag

This is the twenty-first century, so this messenger bag is perfect for a computer laptop. It's a unisex bag that goes anywhere with anyone. The weathered camouflage fabric, multitude of pockets, and multitasking strap all walked into the house on a pair of pants.

Select cargo pants with a lot of pockets for this fun and funky messenger bag.

Materials:

1 pair camouflage pants

½ yd. craft fleece

Sewing thread

2 brass grommets

Brass rings, snaps and chain

3 magnetic snaps

Pressing sheet

Tip:

Select polyester thread for strength and use clear (or smoke-colored) polyester thread for areas of less stress.

69

1

Instructions:

Front and back of the bag

1 For the front of the bag, pick an area on the pants with a great pocket. If you want the bag to hold a laptop, measure the laptop and add 2" around the perimeter. Mark that measurement, and cut.

Begin with a pair of camouflage pants.

Tip:

Personalize the bag by adding a design to the pocket. Add your initials or a message, and consider using the motif provided. Trace the motif onto quilting tracing paper, place the paper over the fabric or pocket, and use the free-motion technique to follow the lines. Tear the paper away and go over the lines again.

Cut the pants apart.

Open the leg.

Cut to fit.

2 For the back of the bag, use a plain section of the leg and cut a small pocket from the back of the pants. When cutting the smaller pocket, leave at least ½" around the sides and bottom. If possible, leave 1½" across the top.

3 Place the front and back of the bag with RST. Sew the sides and bottom with a ½" seam allowance. Sew another line of stitching next to the first. This will ensure the strength needed to carry a laptop around.

4 Box the corners. Measure 1" from the point, and it will result in a 2" width at the corners.

Cut a back piece.

Cut a strap from the waistband.

Cut along the finished edge of the waistband

Attach grommets and swivel snaps.

Strap

1 Create the strap from the waistband.

Cut parallel to the band in a width that will make carrying the bag comfortable and include the belt loops. If the waistband is wide enough, cut along the finished edge and include the belt loops.

2 Measure to see how much additional length you might need for the strap.

3 Measure the width of the waistband/strap, double it, and add 1" to allow for a ½" seam allowance on both edges. Use that measurement to piece leftover fabrics together and create fabric for additional length. Fold the ½" seam allowance on both long lengths to the wrong side of the fabric; pin, and press. Do the same for the short ends. Place one of the short ends around one of the ends of the waistband. Sew across the width to attach. Sew along the pinned edges. Add a second line of stitching to mimic the original stitching on the pants.

4 Send the waistband end of the strap through a metal ring. Fold to the back of the strip, sew in place close to the edge. Backstitch when beginning and ending to secure.

5 Apply two grommets to the other end of the strap. Attach a swivel snap to each grommet. Attach the swivel snaps to a metal ring.

Loops and Closure

1 For the loops, cut two pieces of camo fabric 5" x 5". Fold in half with RST, and sew the long length with a ½" seam allowance. Turn right-side out and press. Place the loops through the strap rings, bring the ends together, and sew the edges together to hold in place.

2 For the closure, create a strip to go around the top of the bag that will hold the three sets of magnetic snaps.

Cut two strips of camo fabric; use the measurement of the width of the bag (plus a 1" seam allowance) for the length and 5" for the width. Place the strips with RST, and sew the short ends with a ½" seam allowance. Fold the length of the band in half with RST and press. Divide the space on each half into thirds, mark, and apply the snaps.

3 Use the dimensions of the bag to cut two pieces of lining fabric. Add pockets to the right side of the fabric, if you like. Use a permanent marking pen to write the words of your favorite song on to the lining.

4 Place the lining fabrics with RST, and sew the sides and bottom. Box the corners.

5 Place the lining inside the camo bag with WST. Check the fit of the lining. Pin together around the opening.

6 Place the strap loops at the side seams on the outside of the bag. Line up the loop edges with the opening.

Tip:

A kit containing matching swivel snaps, chain, and metal rings (split key chain rings) is available in different metal finishes.

Create straps.

Create a strip to hold the magnetic straps.

73

7 Place the closure strip around the opening of the bag with RST.

Line up the side seams and the raw edges at the opening of the bag. Pin and sew with a ½" seam allowance. Trim and finish the edges with a zigzag stitch or serge.

8 Add embellishment with rings and snaps.

Line up the loop edges with the opening, and place the closure strip around the opening of the bag. (The snaps are on the inside.)

Add rings and snaps.

Erica Purse

Embellish a purchased handbag and add a special touch to make a one-of-a-kind design. When you pick out something you already love, it can only get better. Decide whether you want to glam it up with feathers, rhinestones and ribbons, or rock it with black leather and metallic studs. Then, check out the construction of the handbag to see where and how everything will be attached. Lay out all your finery, and audition the items solo and in layers in monochromatic groupings and contrasting bravado. Use a digital camera to photograph the layouts. Place them all in an album. You'll be able to select the best scenario at a glance and archive the rest for future projects.

This sleek, stylish handbag started out perfectly with its on trend trim the color of prized Chinese turquoise. The neutral color and straw texture of the body matched up well with the natural, warm gold of the feathers. The feathers added tactile texture while the flecks of gray, white, and black added visual texture. The small scale animal print with ombre background and black markings added an understated elegance in perfect scale. Of course, this was only one option of many.

Materials:

1 handbag

Feather fringe, the length needed to go
  around the bag — select a trim that is
  not wider than the bag is long.

Animal-print fabric — select a fabric
  that doesn't fray easily. A micro-fiber
  brushed faux fur with a knit backing
  was lightweight, thin, not stretchy, and
  did not ravel when cut.

Hand sewing needle

Thread to match the fabric

Craft glue with instant grab

Sewing thread

Liquid seam sealant (optional)

Instructions:

1 Cut the length of feather fringe needed. Add a dot of glue or a small piece of tape on the ends to keep the feather fringe from raveling.

2 Cut a strip of faux fur fabric to cover the ribbon that holds all the feathers. Cut it the same length as the feather fringe plus 1".

3 Measure the width of the ribbon. Multiply that measurement by three. Use that measurement as the width of the faux fur strip (in this case, 1½").

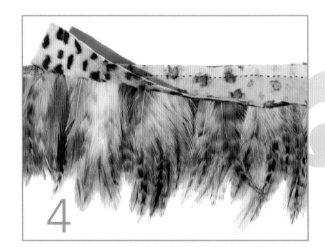

Begin with a plain straw bag.

Choose leopard print and feathers for a lively twist.

Pin and sew the faux fur to the feather fringe.

4 Place the right side of the faux fur strip with the front of the feather fringe ribbon, and line them up evenly at the top. Make sure there is a ½" of the fabric strip that extends past the edge of the feather fringe on each side and pin.

5 Thread the needle with matching thread. Cut a double length of thread and knot the end.

6 Hand sew along the bottom edge of the ribbon to the fabric. Sew from the wrong side of the faux fur fabric with a short running stitch.

7 Place a dot of glue at each end of the strip, and fold the ends to the back of the feather fringe strip. Finger press in place.

8 Place dots of glue along the entire length of the back of the feather fringe.

9 Fold the strip over to the wrong side of the feather fringe, and finger press in place.

10 Run a bead of glue across the front of the handbag, and place the trim.

11 Run a bead of glue across the back of the handbag, and place the trim.

12 Cut a small piece of faux fur fabric to cover the front faux closure belt loop. Measure the length and width of the loop, and cut the fabric slightly larger. Glue the edges under, and then glue over the loop.

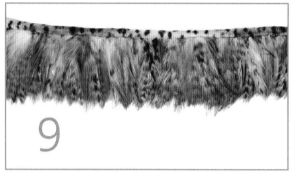

Fold the fabric strip over the feather fringe.

Place the trim on the handbag.

Front of the purse.

Back of the purse.

Antoinette

This petite clutch with rich, elegant striped fabric reminiscent of the opulence of Chateau de Versailles is the perfect foundation for more adornment. The oversized bow was removed. A strip of scalloped bridal lace (the width of the clutch) was tea dyed. Satin ribbon (the color of the lace) is sewn or glued to the bead fringe tape to cover. The ribbon/fringe is sewn or glued to the scalloped lace edge. Center the lace on the clutch and adhere with glue. Use the same satin ribbon to create two bows and attach to the lace. Voilá!

For a different look, begin with a black and gold brocade purse and add trims, beads and leaves.

Materials:

1 pair overalls

½ yd. prewashed linen fabric with a selection of motifs

1 zipper, as long as the width of the bib

Snap tape, the width of the back suspenders

1 purchased belt with grommets (or make one)

3 sets of silver grommets, size ⁷/₁₆

Clear polyester thread

Sewing thread for the bobbin

Decorative or topstitch thread

3 yd. leather lacing

Denim or topstitch needle

Brush with stiff bristles (or chenille brush)

Free-motion foot (optional)

Save The Earth Overalls

Overalls are as American as denim fabric, and the comfortable fit and organic style is high fashion now. Plus, there are pockets, straps, and so many places to embellish. As parts wear out, just add a patch! It will build character as well as convey a message. Make this overall versatile by adding a separating zipper to the bib and snaps to make the suspenders removable. They turn into pants!

Begin with a pair of bib overalls.

Instructions:

Embellish the Bib and Suspenders

1 Select and cut motifs from the linen. Leave ¼" of fabric around the motif.

Select motifs from the linen.

2 Place a motif on the bib, and thread the sewing machine with clear polyester thread and sewing thread to match the fabric in the bobbin. Use a free-motion or straight stitch to sew around the motif, leaving ¼" around the edge of the fabric.

Sew around the motif, leaving ¼" around the edges.

3 Use a stiff brush to brush the edges of the linen to create a soft, chenille edge. Repeat steps 2 and 3 for other motifs.

4 Thread the sewing machine with decorative thread and use the free-motion technique to stipple a design around portions of the bib.

Stipple a design around the bib.

5 Using a disappearing ink pen, write a message, Save the Earth, at the top of the bib. Using a marking pen that doesn't bleed (test it on an inside seam), cover the disappearing ink and then go over the edges with a darker color pen. If the marking pen requires heat to set, do that with a pressing cloth.

Write a message on the bib.

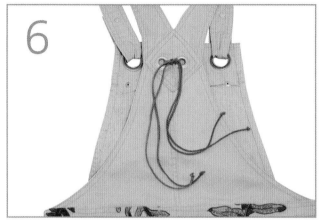
Add two grommets on the back.

6 Add two grommets on the back of the suspenders. Cut two lengths of leather lacing, thread through the grommets, and tie. Knot the ends of the lacings.

Cut two lengths of leather lacings and tie at the tab on the bib. Knot the ends.

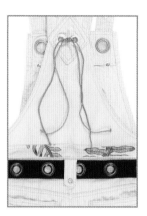
Front and back of the bib.

Alter the Waistband

1 Cut the bib off the front of the coveralls.

Leave at least ½" of fabric on the waistband. Use a zigzag stitch to finish that edge the edge on the bib.

Then, fold the zigzagged edges to the wrong side, and stitch in place close to the edge.

Cut the bib off the overalls

2 Place one side of the zipper front behind the front edge of the bib, and pin and/or baste in place. Consider using a zipper foot to sew close to the edge of the teeth.

Finish the edge.

3 Place the other side of the zipper behind the waistband. Pin and/or baste in place. Topstitch close to the edge of the waistband.

Consider sewing over the existing topstitching. Topstitch again about ¼" from the previous topstitching.

Topstitch the zipper in place.

4 Cut the overall suspenders in the back away from the waistband, leaving about ½" of fabric above it. Use a zigzag stitch to finish the edges on both sides.

 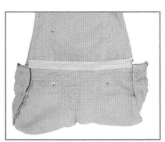

The front.   *The back side.*

5 Turn the edge above the waistband over to the wrong side. Pin and stitch in place.

6 Mark a line ½" from the bottom edge of the suspenders, and cut. Measure the width at the cut.

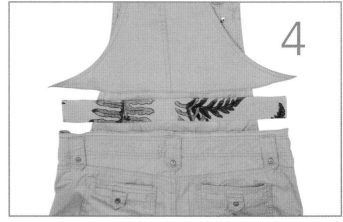

Cut the overall suspenders away from the waistband.

7 Use the measurement above plus 1" (for side seam allowances) as the length to create a band. Use 3" as the width. Fold the length of the band in half with RST, which will result in a width of 1½". Sew the short ends with a ½" seam allowance. Turn right-side out and press. Topstitch the short ends close to the edge. Use a zigzag stitch to finish the length of the raw edges.

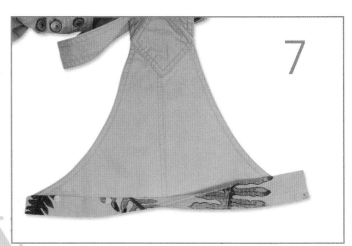

Create a band.

8 Place the zigzag edge and the back suspender edge with right sides together and pin. Sew with a ½" seam allowance, and press all the seams down toward the band. Topstitch the edge of the band, catching the seam allowances underneath.

9 Cut a length of snap tape, set along the print band, pin, and sew along the edges of the tape.

10 Place the remaining snap tape on wrong side of the overall waistband. Sew along the edge of the tape. If some parts of the waistband are too thick for the sewing machine needle to penetrate, sew in place by hand.

Add a Linen Pocket

1 Create a pocket with a finished size of 6" wide x 7" long and a flap 3½" x 6" with a grommet on the lower corner.

2 Create the pocket flap by cutting a rectangle 7" long by 6" wide. Fold in half with WST, and sew around three sides (with raw edges) with a ½" seam allowance. Sew another line of stitching ¼" from the first edge. Apply a grommet in the corner.

3 Create the pocket by cutting a rectangle 12" long by 6" wide. Fold in half with WST, and sew around three sides (with raw edges) with a ½" seam allowance. Sew another line of stitching ¼" from the first. The ½" seam allowances are brushed to fray.

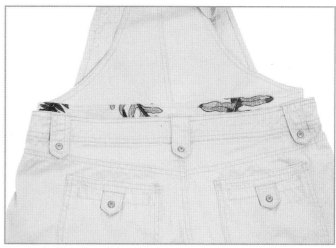

Topstitch the edge of the band.

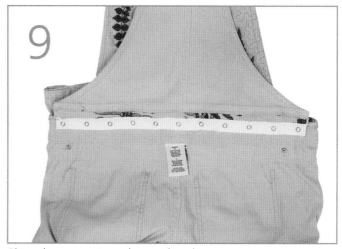

Pin and sew snap tape close to the edge.

Finish the snape tape edges.

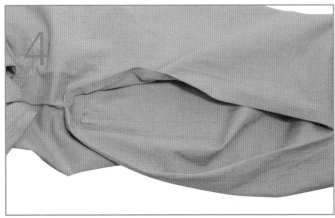

Open the inside seam of the leg.

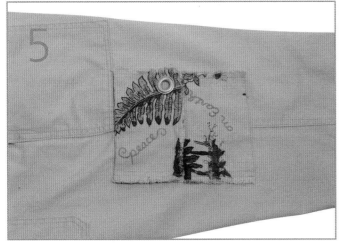

Place the pocket on the leg.

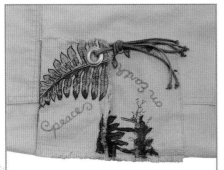

Add leather lacing.

Write a message on the pocket.

4 Open the inside seam of the right leg of the overall around the area that the pocket will be placed. (To determine that, put on the overalls and let your hand drop to the side. Your hand should be able to reach inside the pocket.)

5 Place the pocket over the side seam; pin and stitch the sides and bottom in place. Place the flap about 1" above the top of the pocket. Pin across the top of the flap. Check to be sure you can lift the flap and place your hand in the pocket. Face the flap up, and edge stitch along the finished edge. Let the flap face down over the pocket opening.

6 Cut two lengths of leather lacing, thread through the grommet, and tie. Tie a knot at the ends of the lacing. Write a message on the pocket. Test the marker on a scrap of linen first. Press if needed to set the marker.

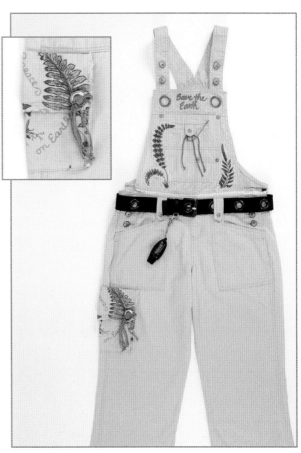

Materials:

1 pair of hightop sneakers

Colorful alphabet beads

Foam alphabets with adhesive backs

Small beads in assorted colors

Flower-shaped acrylic crystals

1 yd. green organza ribbon, 1½" wide

1 yd. green grosgrain ribbon, ½" wide

Hand sewing needle

Clear polyester thread

Black permanent marker

Waterproof fabric glue

1"-wide brush

Small screwdriver

1 fat quarter of cotton fabric for shoe
    lining (optional)

Spring Espadrilles

Jump into spring with shoes you can design while waiting for the snow to thaw. Celebrate with color and words of inspiration. Leftover scrapbooking items are perfect for the sneakers, and the organza ribbon adds a bright splash of color to these festive footsies.

Begin with a pair of hightop sneakers.

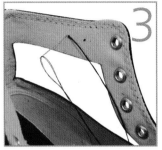

Add beads to the shoes with needle and thread.

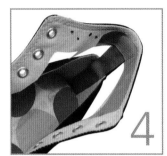

Cover the spine with ribbon.

Tip:

If the inside of the shoe is not pretty, cover it with cheerful cotton fabric. Place the shoe on the wrong side of the fabric and cut the shape, adding ½" extra. Place the fabric with the right side down inside the shoe. Smooth the fabric to the perimeter of the shoe. Use a pencil to mark the perimeter. Pull the fabric out and place on the remainder of the fabric with RST. Cut both layers ¼" outside of the penciled line. Brush the inside of the foot area with waterproof fabric glue. Carefully, place the fabric inside the shoe, right-side up. Start with the heel and slowly smooth to the toe. Tuck the extra ¼" of fabric between the sole and the sides of the shoe. Use a small screw driver to push the edge of the fabric down.

Instructions:

1 Look inside the shoe, and use the construction of the shoe to decide what will be cut away to form the espadrille. Some parts are needed to keep the shoe together. The "tongue" under the lacing was cut away. The spine above the heel was needed, so the sides were cut away leaving as much fabric as possible to support the area near the lacing.

2 Mark the area to be cut away with a chalk pencil. Cut the fabric with a pair of sharp scissors. Use a black permanent marker to color the edge of the fabric that was cut away to match the outside of the sneaker.

3 Add words such as Live, Love and Laugh with beads. Thread the needle with a double length of thread, and make a substantial knot at the end.

Use the chalk pencil to mark the placement of the "words". Send the threaded needle from the inside of the shoe, and thread a bead, a couple of alphabets, another bead, and send the needle back inside the shoe and tie a knot. Send the needle back out, add more colored beads and alphabet beads, and then send the needle back to the inside and knot. Knotting after a few beads and alphabets gives more stability to the beads. Do the same for the other shoe.

4 Use a length of grosgrain ribbon to cover the thread knots at the spine and heel of the shoe.

Then use another length of ribbon horizontally to cover the knots along the sides. Apply the glue from edge to edge on the ribbon so they lie flat and do not curl and rub the inside of your foot.

5   Peel the paper backing off the foam alphabets and place a message on the rubber toe of the sneaker.

6   Peel the paper backing off the jewel flowers and place along the sides of the shoe.

The jewels come in several sizes and colors, so mix them up and place them randomly. Once you are sure of the placement, place quick-grab glue on the backs of the embellishments and replace.

7   Before cutting the length of organza ribbon, thread it through the grommets on the front of the shoe. Don't send the ribbon through every grommet, and tie where comfortable.

8   Journal and write secrets inside the shoe…no one looks in there!

Journal on the inside of the shoe.

Bombay Jewels

Add elegance to a pair of slip-on shoes with clear crystal jewels. If the toe of the shoe already has a design, use it to your advantage; it will help you line up the crystals. Apply hot-fix flat-back jewels, which will stay in place immediately. The crystal applicator comes with a tip with a larger, round, flat surface. Use this tip to hold the crystal against the shoe and activate the glue.

Something BLUE

Reach For The Stars Jacket

Everyone loves the color blue. After all, it's the color of the sky and the sea. Blue is a color on our beloved flag as well as our national fabric: denim. Denim is the great equalizer of age, season, socio-economic standing, and style. Surely there is some denim in your closet that can be revved up or cut. If not, a trip to the thrift store will certainly help you find some treasure. Check out the children's section for jeans and overalls with cute little pockets, embroidery and grommets. The men's section offers jeans that are soft and frayed. The teen section will be full of designer denim skirts that are so short that they are ready to be bags. And don't forget to pick up some "camo" while you are there!

Create artful artwear with uplifting themes. Remember, you are wearing powerful subliminal messages for all the world to see and appreciate. Use artistic calligraphy to blend in with swirl designs punctuated with metallic hot fix star studs. Adorn your pockets with acrylic Marquis-cut jewels; add grommets and leather lacings for embellishment; and soften everything with faux fur fabric trim on the collar and cuffs. The juxtaposition of exciting textures and the inspirational messages are certain to set you in altered stellar style.

Materials:

1 denim jacket

¼ yd. faux leopard fabric

Fleur-de-lis metal pronged studs

Silver and gold hot-fix metal star studs

Acrylic sew-on jewels

24 sets of grommets

2 yd. leather lacing

Denim or topstitch needle

Clear polyester thread

Hand sewing needle

Pencil and disappearing ink pen

Spray adhesive

Make the collar edge.

Add two rows of grommets to the back.

Tip:

Cut the hole slightly smaller than needed. This will allow for a tighter grip around the grommet shaft.

Instructions:

1 Cut the faux leopard fabric ¼" larger than the collar and cuff. Turn the edges of the faux fur under and leave the denim edge showing.

Use spray adhesive to hold the fabric in place. Use clear polyester thread in the machine and in the bobbin. Use a zigzag stitch or straight stitch to sew the edge of the faux leopard fabric to the collar. Use the same method for the cuff.

2 Use the disappearing ink pen to mark where the acrylic jewels will be placed. Place a dot of repositional craft glue on the back of the jewels to hold them in place. This glue allows you to change your mind during the design process. When you are pleased with the design, thread the needle with clear polyester thread and sew the jewels in place.

3 When embellishing the back of the jacket, use the stitching as a guide for grommet placement. Place them equidistant and in rows along the stitching. Use a pencil to trace the inside of the grommet hole, and use sharp scissors or a punch set to cut the hole. Place two rows of grommets, and lace with leather strips.

4 Use a black permanent marker to add a message and artistic swirls to the jacket. Use a calligraphy style with flourish so the message is subliminal and in keeping with the flow of the design.

5 Use the crystal-setting tool with the flat hot spot tip to apply sprays of hot-fix star studs. They are quick and easy to apply and offer immediate gratification.

6 Add larger fleur-de-lis studs with prongs.

Tip:

The pointed prongs sink easily into fabric and stay in place when bent. Remove them before laundering, or wash carefully by hand.

Add calligraphy.

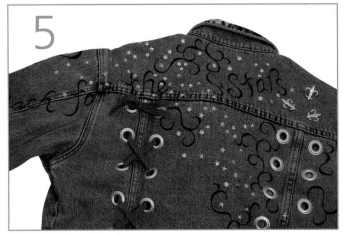

Apply hot-fix star studs.

Add fleur-de-lis studs.

Front of the jacket.

Back of the jacket.

91

Joie De Vivre

The colors and designs on this jacket were inspired by the gossamer dimensional appliqués and metallic Papillion (or butterflies). The expressive colors, textures and movement of line just makes you want to kick up your heels and dance!

Materials:

1 denim jacket

Iron-on dimensional appliqués

Iron-on metallic butterfly

Polyester embroidery thread in
    turquoise and lime green

4 turquoise safety pins

8 Swarovski crystal beads, 8 mm

½ yd. tear-away stabilizer

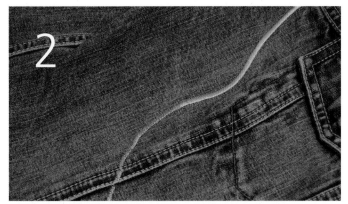

Satin stitch meandering lines.

Satin stitch meandering lines on the back and front.

Place the butterfly on the back.

Instructions:

1 Audition the placement of the appliqués and butterfly in different places on the jacket. When pleased, pin them in place.

2 Use a chalk pencil to mark the placement of the meandering lines, or create impromptu meandering lines. Satin stitch these lines with turquoise thread.

3 Alternate thread colors to create contrasting satin stitched lines. Use two layers of tear-away stabilizer underneath the lines.

Leave room for the butterfly on the back.

4 Place the embroidered motifs on the jacket and press with a pressing cloth. Check the manufacturer's instructions for application specifications.

5 The butterfly design for the back is sand-wiched between two layers of clear plastic. Peel away the plastic underneath the butterfly. Place the butterfly on the fabric, and finger press to adhere temporarily. Follow manufacturer's instructions to set. Peel away the remaining plastic.

6 Embellish with safety pins and crystals. These are awesome "last-minute" items that take the design element over the top.

Place a crystal bead on the safety pin, weave the pin through the collar fabric, add another crystal bead, and close the pin.

Celebrity Signature Handbag

Denim is the perfect match for the ultra-stylish leopard print. Animal skin is the new black with attitude. This project allows you to alter the size and colors of the leopard spots with a bold allover print or understated minimal effect. Real leather and suede were used to create these, but feel free to substitute faux leather, upholstery fabric or any non-fray fabric. Use permanent glue or the free-motion technique to anchor the pieces.

Tip:

Determine what size bag you will make. For a small, narrow bag, look for a child's denim skirt or jeans. For a larger tote, use an adult skirt or jeans. Look for a style where the front and back waist are similar in depth (The low-riser style has a lower front and higher back. This makes it difficult to have a bag that lies flat and is even across the top.) Refer to The East Meets West Skirt on page 109 to see how to turn denim jeans into a skirt.

Materials:

1 pair denim jeans or skirt

½ yd. lining fabric

½ yd. fusible craft fleece (or batting)

Sewing thread to match

Clear polyester thread

1 pair of purse handles

¼ yd. 3"-wide lace

6" square of black kid leather

6" square of saddle kid suede

Permanent glue

Fray check

Lay the jeans or skirt flat.

Instructions:

1. If using jeans, cut and piece jeans to lie flat and measure 16" from the top of the waistband. Mark with a chalk pencil, and cut.

   Lay the skirt or pieced jeans flat. Cut the bottom edge using a ruler for a straight edge.

2. Turn inside-out, and sew across the bottom with a ½" seam allowance. Press the seams open. Box the corners. Turn right-side out.

3. Place the lace around the curve of one of the pockets. If the lace does not "ease" into a curve, cut a few of the connecting threads in the lace design. Just before you cut, place a small drop of fray check on those connecting threads.

4. Pin the lace down the center. Place adhesive down the center of the wrong side of the lace, and press in place. Work in 1" or 2" increments out to the sides.

Place the lace on the bag.

Tip:

Instead of adhesive, use free-motion stitching with clear polyester thread to sew the lace in place. In that case, pin it all in place and sew before sewing the bottom of the denim bag.

Make the spots.

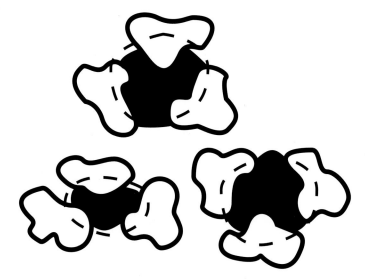

Cut leather spots using the photo as a guide. Use as many sets of spots as needed. Cut the center "spot" out of the saddle-colored suede. Each spot uses two or three black leather "squiggles." Occasionally, in place of a squiggle, use a black leather "dot." Cut as many sets as desired.

6 Place the spots, squiggles and dots on the other side of the bag. When you are satisfied with the design placement, carefully take one set apart and apply glue. Glue the spots first, and then the squiggles and dots. Be sure to place glue all the way to the edges.

7 Fold the lining fabric with RST. Lay the denim bag on the fabric, and cut the lining in the same shape, allowing for seam allowances all the way around.

8 Cut the fleece the same size as the lining, EXCEPT make it 1" narrower at each side seam so there will be less bulk in the side seams.

9 Spray adhesive on one side of each of the fleece pieces, and lay the wrong side of each of the lining pieces on the batting. Hand press in place.

Tip:

If you aren't sure you will remember how it all goes back together (after placement), use a chalk pencil to outline the pieces. Glue all the sets.

Tip:

For a quilted lining, center the batting on the wrong side of the lining, and quilt using your favorite quilting pattern.

7

Lay the bag on the lining fabric to determine measurements.

12

Create handle loops.

13

Put loops through handles.

Tip:

If there is a denim belt loop or the front button in the way as you stitch, sew as far as you can, backstitch and stop, cut the threads and continue on the other side. You may have to hand stitch in just a few places. Be sure that the loops are sewn by machine and reinforced.

10 Place the lining/batting pieces with RST and sew the sides and bottom with a ½" seam allowance. (Place the lining bag inside the denim bag with WST. If the lining has a lot of folds and is still too big, take it in at the sides and bottom.) Remove the lining from the bag. Fold the top edge of the lining to the wrong side, and edge stitch.

11 Place the mark in the center, 2" from the top edge. Mark a dot for placing magnetic snaps on each side of the lining. (Make sure the placement is not too close to the top edge, or it could be difficult to sew the lining to the denim bag.) Apply one side of the snap to each dot.

12 Cut four 5½"-wide x 4"-long strips for the handle loops. (This works for hardware that is 2" wide. If the fabric is very lightweight, use a double layer of fabric or back with a leave-in stabilizer.) Fold the width of the strip in half with RST, and sew the length with a ½" seam allowance. Press the seam open. Turn the loop right-side out, and place the seam in the center. Press and do the same for the remaining three strips.

13 Place a loop through each of the handle hardware and fold in half with the seams facing each other. Pin and sew close to the edge to keep ends together.

14 Place the lining inside the denim bag with WST, and pin in place around the opening.

15 Place the handle loops in between the lining and the denim bag. Center the handles on the bag. Thread the sewing machine and the bobbin with clear polyester thread, and sew the lining edge to the denim waistband.

Savannah Shoulder Bag

You can't have too many of these denim shoulder bags, since they are quick, easy to make and inexpensive. Use the dimensions provided, or alter the pattern for a smaller or larger bag. The best part of this project is collecting all the wonderful trim. Make a few of these to use up the trim!

Tip:

Tapestry fabric is a perfect match for denim because they share the same density and stabilizers won't be necessary. If you want to use a lightweight fabric, consider pre-quilting the fabric or backing it with stabilizer.

The dimensions for the base of the bag (in this case, the brown tapestry fabric) and the lining is provided. The size of the denim piece for the front of the bag will depend on what you use. If you choose a child's garment, more details, such as pockets, zippers and loops, will fit. If using an adult's garment, just a few details may fit (or make a bigger bag).

Three types of closures are used on this bag: a large sew-on snap, a snap applied with prongs and a magnetic snap. Feel free to use all three, or just use the ones you prefer. Refer to the technique section for the application instructions.

Materials:

1 pair of denim jeans

½ yd. tapestry fabric

½ yd. lining fabric

6" x 10" piece of silk fabric for bow

6" length of beaded fringe

Assortment of trims

1 set of sew-on snaps

1 set of snaps with prongs

1 set of magnetic snaps

Sewing thread

Decorative thread

Clear polyester thread

Denim needle

Instructions:

Preparation

Tip:

Pattern #1: Use the dimensions with the solid lines for base. Pattern #2: Use the dimensions with the dashed lines for lining. Pattern #3: Use the dimensions with the dotted lines. Consider using this method when creating linings for other bags.

1 Refer to the pattern on page 103. Use Pattern #1 to cut two pieces of tapestry fabric and two pieces of craft fleece. Use Pattern #2 to cut two pieces of fabric for the lining. Use Pattern #3 to cut one denim piece. Spray one side of each piece of craft fleece and place that side on the wrong side of each piece of tapestry.

Tip:

Use strong sewing thread whenever possible, and clear polyester thread when a matching thread will show. When using the clear polyester thread in places of stress, sew another line of stitching to secure.

Cut tapestry and craft fleece.

Back Pocket

1 Cut along the sides and bottom edge of one of the back pockets.

Cut away the inside of the pocket.

2 Place the back pocket on a tapestry/fleece piece. (The narrow end of the tapestry piece is the top.) Place it on an angle, pin, and sew in place close to the edges along the sides and bottom. Use the clear polyester thread and a zigzag stitch.

3 Add a set of snaps with prongs to the pocket. The hardware is a great addition to the denim.

Tip:

Embellish the back pocket by adding thick, rich satin stitching with decorative thread. Place two layers of lightweight stabilizers underneath the area to be embellished. Use a chalk pencil to create a decorative line, or follow the existing stitching on the pocket. Use a wide satin stitch to create a dramatic line. Carefully tear the stabilizer away.

Cut close to the finished edge of the pocket.

View from inside.

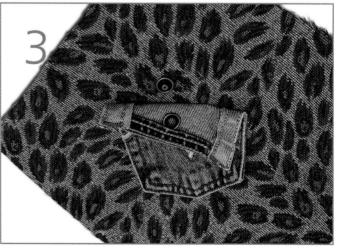

Add snaps to the pocket.

Front Pocket

1 Center the denim piece on the other tapestry/
fleece piece, and pin. Be sure to place it at
least 1½" from the top of the tapestry piece.
Use the clear polyester thread and a zigzag
stitch to sew close to the edges on the sides
and bottom. Add some color by sewing a few
wiggles of satin stitching in the left bottom
corner. Use the same thread as on the back
pocket.

2 Add a set of sew-on snaps to the inside of
the jeans pocket and the tapestry. Refer to
the techniques section. (These snaps are great
because none of the application stitches will
be seen.)

3 Place the two tapestry pieces with RST, pin
along the sides and bottom, and sew with a
½" seam allowance. If the tapestry is loosely
woven, sew another line of stitching in the
seam allowance ⅛" from the first. Box the
corners.

Add snaps to the inside of the pocket.

Optional Inside Pockets

1 Cut two 9"-long x 12"-wide pieces from the
lining fabric. Cut two 4"-long x 12"-wide
pieces of fleece. Fold the length of the lining
piece in half with RST, and place one layer of
fleece underneath (keeping the 12" width).
Do the same for the other pocket piece.
Sew along the long edges with a ½" seam
allowance. Turn right-side out, and press,
essentially creating tubes.

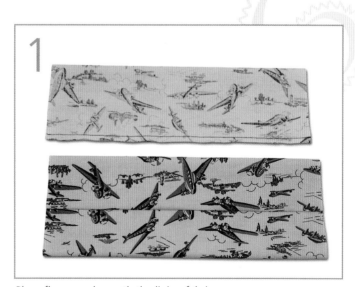

Place fleece underneath the lining fabric.

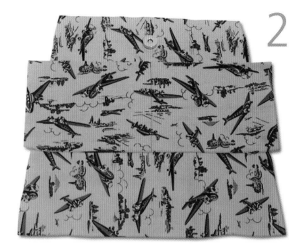

Place a pocket on each lining piece.

2 Place one pocket on each lining piece. Place them horizontally 3" from the top or 3" from the bottom and pin in place.

3 Stitch along the bottom edge of the pockets and down the center. Cut the excess from the sides to fit the shape of the lining. Sew the sides of the pocket to the sides of the lining close to the edge.

Lining

1 Place the two lining pieces with RST, pin the sides and bottom, and then sew with a ½" seam allowance. Box the corners.

2 Add a magnetic snap to the lining. Mark the center of the lining 1½" from the top edge. Apply the magnetic snaps to each side of the lining.

3 Turn the top edge (½") of the lining to the wrong side, and edge stitch. Place the lining inside the denim bag with WST. Place and pin the lining edge below the tapestry edge.

Tip:

The pockets near the top are convenient, but if your keys and cell phone are heavy, they will pull the top of the bag down.

Strap

1 Create a long shoulder strap with the tapestry fabric. The finished strap is 48". Cut the fabric 50" long and 5" wide. Piece fabrics together if needed. Fold the width of the long strip in half with WST. Tuck the raw edges on the long side under ½", pin, and stitch close to the edge. Place the ends of the strap between the lining and the denim bag at the sides, and pin in place.

Tuck edges under ½" and pin.

Sew straps in place on the bag.

Finish the Bag

1 Thread the sewing machine and bobbin with clear polyester thread, and sew the lining to the denim bag. If some sections are blocked by belt loops, stop, and finish sewing by hand.

2 Add a wild trim with hand painted and carved discs dangling form a grosgrain ribbon. The discs on this trim were far apart so tucks were sewn to fill a small space with more discs. The ribbon was folded in the center between discs and sewn ½" from the folded edge.

3 Cut a length of the altered ribbon and trim to fit the width of the front denim piece. Turn the beginning and end of the ribbon under and sew to the edge of the denim with a zigzag stitch using the clear polyester thread.

4 Add a silken bow. Fold the silk rectangle in half with RST, keeping the 10" width. Sew the short sides and the long length with a ½" seam allowance. Leave a 2" opening in the center of the long length to turn through.

5 Trim the seams, cut the corners on the diagonal and turn through the opening. Tuck the seam allowance inside and press. Tie the bow once in the center.

Glue or hand stitch the bow and bead fringe to the front of the bag.

5

Leave a 2" opening.

Tie the bow in the center.

Pattern #1 (solid), Pattern #2 (dash) and Pattern #3 (dots)

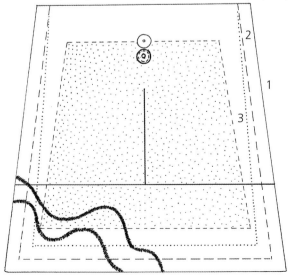

Enlarge pattern at 200%.

A Geisha's Journal Vest

The Geisha writes of unrequited love of a man beyond her reach. She keeps a journal masked in the style of a puzzling Haiku. Who knows? Her memoirs could one day become a best-selling novel!

Decide on a theme and gather all the supplies. Crop fabrics and frame them with fabric strips. Use bias-cut meandering strips to lead the focus from vignette to vignette. A sprinkling of baubles and beads add drama and sewing techniques add layered texture.

Back the fabrics with batting and quilt following the lines. Embellish with hand sewn beads. Frame smaller bits of fabric with fabric strips using the log cabin piecing technique. Back the pieced squares

with thin, pre-washed flannel. Cut ½" strips on the bias. Place cording or fabric through the hang hole of a charm, and sew in place. Mark the corner placement of the items on the back of the vest with a chalk pencil. Meander the bias strip from one motif to the other. Pin and baste in place. Sew ⅛" from the edge on both sides of the bias strip. Place the motifs, and sew around the perimeter close to the edges. Use two rows of stitching next to each other. If satin stitching, stitch one row, and then cover with satin stitching. Use a wide stitch width to maximize the drama and shimmer of the thread.

Free-motion lines placed side by side were used to outline the crane and peony. Swarovski crystals embellish the peony. A hand-sewn "x" was used to quilt and add color to the small framed bamboo image. The circle cut-out technique decorates the left shoulder, and a purchased pin adds sparkle to the collar.

Materials:

1 denim vest

½ yd. fabrics with Asian motifs

Batting

¼ yd. tear-away stabilizer

Assorted coins, charms and brooches

Decorative threads

Hand sewing needle

Tip:

Use a digital camera to save all the auditions.

Instructions:

Preparation

1 Audition pieces of fabric, embellishments and trims on the vest. If it helps, make a sketch of the vest and place the shapes of the items that will be added. It will give you an idea of the size, shape and placement that would be visually appealing.

Large Images

1 Start with the most significant (or largest) items. The image of the Geisha writing in her journal is the inspiration for this vest. The large image is placed on the back of the vest to allow more space to continue the story. Cut desired shape and pin in place.

A small Geisha is selected for the front to entice the viewer and give a hint of what is to come. In honor of the Geisha, peonies, the auspicious crane, and bamboo grace the front. These pieces are fussy cut from quilting cotton and backed with batting, then placed on a large layer of leave-in stabilizer.

Begin with the main item.

2 Select and enhance some of the lines with decorative thread.

Enhance the lines with decorative thread.

I laid this piece on the denim to make it easier to see. This is the view of the crane and peony piece from the back of the piece. The thread shows most of the outlining is done, the batting is trimmed from the edge, and some of the leave-in stabilizer is trimmed away (near the far right).

Fussy cut around the edges of the motif, spray a small amount of adhesive on the back, and place it on the vest. This will keep the motif in place temporarily and allow you to reposition it. Do this for the Geisha on the back and the front, and the peonies with the crane.

Square Frame

1 Create interest with log cabin frames surrounding special fabrics. Three small pieces of fabric from vintage kimonos are showcased with log cabin frames on the back of the vest.

Tips:

Leave-in stabilizer is a lightweight, non-woven product that helps to stabilize but doesn't add bulk. When used under the batting, it allows you to emphasize the lines of the peonies and crane with lustrous thread and free motion quilting. The softness of the stabilizer will encourage the fabric and thread to "shrink up", create loft, and results in a more dramatic dimension of quilting, similar to Trapunto. By embellishing most of the fabric separately and placing more of the same stabilizer under that area of the vest, there is less risk of distorting a section of your garment. When applying to the garment, place tear-away stabilizer underneath the vest and keep the stitching minimal. Outline the motif and add a few lines evenly through the interior. Too many lines will make it difficult to remove the tear-away stabilizer.

Trapunto is a quilting technique that originated in Italy in the 16th century. Its popularity in the United States began in the late 1700's. Typically, appliqué shapes were stuffed with batting, which resulted in a raised surface.

1

Choose three pieces of vintage fabric.

2

Use the log cabin piecing technique.

The first piece is a brightly colored silk fabric taken from a young girl's kimono. The bright colors signify the days of apprenticeship when the Geisha started as a Maiko. The second piece is from a brocade obi that might have been worn by a Geisha. The third fabric was taken from the lining of a Haori (kimono-shaped jacket) worn over a kimono. These squares are framed with cotton fabric with swish lines that represent the weave of textiles. The auspicious bamboo motif is placed on the front and framed to echo the frames on the back.

2 Use a log cabin piecing technique with strips that are 1¼" wide to frame the small squares. Decide on the placement, and mark with chalk lines in the corners.

Bias Strip

1 Create the red and white bias strip by using a rotary cutter and ruler to cut 1"-wide strips on the bias.

Cut about two yards to be sure you have enough fabric. The red and white cotton fabric design represents the traditional Japanese Shibori (fabric manipulation and dyeing) technique, and it is an essential part of Japanese textiles. The red color directs the eye from vignette to vignette. Once the major pieces and placement have been determined, set the path of the meandering red strip. Create subtle curves.

Sharp, deep curves will create puckering. Lay the strip loosely, and do not stretch it as it is pinned. Stitch ⅛" from the edge. Use a brush to brush the edges carefully and create a soft fray.

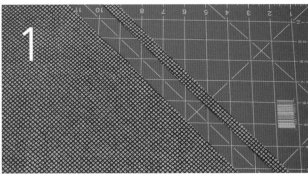

Cut strips.

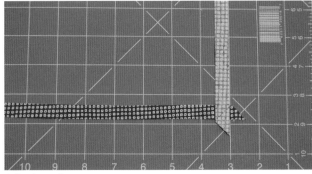

Join the strips.

2 Tie an Asian charm to a length of red bias, and hang it under the Geisha motif on the back. Replace the motifs in their marked area.

Thread and Bead Embellishment

1 Use straight stitching with black thread close to the raw edges of the long cabin squares.

2 Use straight stitching lines with pink thread close to the raw edges of the large Geisha. Sew over two of the lines with satin stitching.

3 Use straight stitching lines with metallic gold thread close to the raw edges of the Geisha on the front. Sew over two lines with satin stitching.

4 Adding a spray of red beads is another way of directing the eye. Hand sew the beads in a spray arrangement to lead them to the red and white circle on the shoulder.

5 Add a dimensional circle cutout on the shoulder.

2

Create meandering curves. Mark the design placement with chalk.

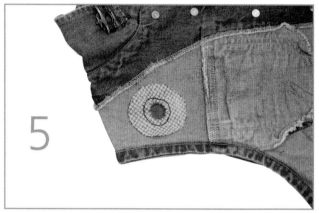

5

Place the circle on the inside.

Complete the circle.

Front of the vest.

Back of the vest.

East Meets West Skirt

The all-American denim meets chiffon with Japanese design motifs. How apropos for this designer/author! Textured black lace, sparkling bling, and a bead belt set the tone for this eclectic altered style. For a one-of-a-kind personal touch, add calligraphy and swirls with a black fabric marker.

Tip:

Venice lace is elegant and has great dimensional detail.

Use beautiful lace.

It is available in almost every width and as yardage. The designs in the lace are connected with delicate connecting threads. When the threads are cut and stabilized, the motifs can be separated and used individually.

Cut the lace apart, if desired.

Materials:

1 pair denim shorts or skirt

3 yd. chiffon (for exact measurement, see step 3)

Black Venice lace, enough to cover skirt perimeter

Hot-fix flat back Swarovski crystals in jewel tones

Smoke-clear polyester thread

Black sewing thread

Black permanent markers

Bead belt

Denim or topstitch needle

Free-motion foot

Liquid seam sealant

Instructions:

Prepare the Denim

1 Cut the shorts to separate the front from the back. Then cut close to the flat felled seam edge far enough to allow everything to lay flat.

Pin in place. Thread the machine with the smoke-clear thread and black sewing thread in the bobbin. Sew close to the flat felled seam edge, catching both layers of fabric. Sew a second seam, or use the zigzag stitch to ensure stability. From the inside, cut away excess fabric.

2 Trim to create an even hemline.

Begin with a pair of denim shorts.

Separate the front from the back.

Trim to create an even hemline.

Prepare the Skirt

1 Create a half-circle pattern, and cut two half circles from the chiffon. Place the sides parallel to the selvage.

2 Place the two half circles with RST, and sew the side seams. Match the side seams of the skirt to the sides of the denim. Ease and pin the rest of the chiffon to the skirt edge with RST. Sew with a ½" seam allowance. Sew the edges with a zigzag stitch or serge to finish.

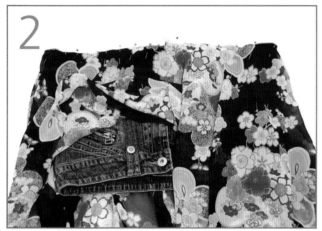

Place the chiffon skirt and denim with RST.

Finish the edges.

Tips:

The amount of fabric needed will be determined by the size of the denim skirt opening and the length of the chiffon skirt. Measure the skirt opening and divide by Pi (3.14) to find the diameter. Divide by 2 to find the radius for the inner circle measurement. Decide on the length of the skirt, and add an inch or two for the hem. Add the radius of the inner circle to the skirt length, and this will be the radius of your outer circle, the chiffon skirt edge.

The swirls have a look similar to calligraphy. Exaggerate the curves by making the curves wider and tapering in. Experiment with different shapes to create your own style.

After trimming the hem, let it hang overnight to allow the weave of the fabric to finish stretching. A loose-woven fabric may stretch a little more.

Lace Embellishment

1 Use lace to cover the edge where the denim meets the chiffon.

2 Use lace yardage, strips or lace appliqués. Plan ahead by placing drops of liquid seam sealant on the connecting threads that will be cut. Let dry, and cut apart. Place the lace in an even strip or in an asymmetrical array.

3 Use adhesive spray or repositional fabric adhesive to hold the lace in place temporarily.

4 Use the smoke-clear thread to sew the lace in place. Consider using the free motion technique with a darning foot (which stays suspended above the throat plate and allows clearance for the denim and lace).

Apply Swarovski crystals to the lace and around the lace motifs.

5 Add messages and swirl designs with a black marker. Mark the swirls with a thin line, and then go back and add flourish.

Trim to create an even edge. Consider using the chalk hem marker. Finish the hem edge with a serged rolled hem. Or, finish the hem with a straight stitch by folding the hem edge to the wrong side and edgestitching. Then, fold again to the wrong side and edgestitch.

Cover the edge of the denim with lace.

Leopards 'n Lace

A long, fitted denim skirt allows for a more dramatic length. Leopard-print georgette fabric (a sheer fabric slightly heavier and more opaque than chiffon) with a width of 60 inches makes a longer, fuller skirt. The inner circle is one and a half times the measurement of the skirt edge. This was to allow for some gathers and a fuller skirt.

1   Create a half circle pattern. Cut two half circles from the fabric, sew the side seams to create a full circle, and finish the seam edges. Sew two lines of stitching (with a longer stitch length of about eight per inch) around the inner circle to gather. Start and stop at each side seam for the front and for the back.

2   Divide the inner circle of the fabric into fourths, and mark with pins.

3   Divide the skirt hem into fourths, and mark with pins. Match the pins of the circle to the skirt with RST. Pull the gathering threads at the side seams, and ease to fit. Pin and/or baste. Use the second thread farthest from the edge of the fabric as a guide, and sew through the layers of fabric and skirt. Trim and zigzag the edges to finish. Place the strip of lace where the fabric and skirt meet. Consider cutting the lace apart for an asymmetrical look. Use spray adhesive on the back of the lace to apply temporarily. When dry, use a smoke (for dark lace) or clear (for white lace) polyester thread to sew the lace to the skirt. Trim the hem evenly, let it hang overnight, and then trim again. Finish with a rolled hem edge on the serger, or use a straight stitch.

I DO!

Chloe's Wedding Dress

This elegant ensemble is both timely and timeless. Not pricey, but priceless. Designing and creating your own gown for such a memorable event is an incredible accomplishment.

By this chapter, you've learned to create what makes you happy. You've learned to use what you can find and not chase the elusive item that might delay your happiness. You have the self confidence to create your own altered style.

Give the dress an extra-long length, and allow it to "puddle" on the floor for a dramatic wedding photo. Add a long sheer belt tied at the waist to create a fitted silhouette, and let the remainder of the belt fall to the floor as the train. A fitted shrug with sleeve flounces to match the belt brings the ensemble together. A charming headpiece with a short veil along with a vintage purse keep the look quaint with a hint of retro style.

Keeping the wedding gown simple allows more time to have fun with the accessories. Chloe's dress is created with two half circles of a lightweight jersey knit. The fabric and altered style create the ultimate drape. It will fit every body. White decorative (rayon or high sheen polyester embroidery) thread has a silken sheen and is perfect for finishing the hem.

Materials:

8 yd. of 60"-wide fabric (yardage will depend on the size and length of the dress)

1" elastic to fit the upper bust

White sewing thread

White decorative thread

Safety pin

Tip:

The upper bust is measured across the chest, under the arms and across the back. This measurement is used for the inner circle. Measure the gown length from the upper bust, over the bust and down to the floor (plus a few inches). You can always cut the excess. For a hem that "puddles", add at least another 10" and more yardage.

Tip:

For the dress, select a jersey knit (which has two-way stretch) for drape and comfort. For the right length, the fabric should be 56" to 60" wide. Do not select a sheer fabric unless you are lining it or creating a slip. If the fabric doesn't stretch, the opening will need to be large enough to put on over the head and arms. This will require the circle opening to be much larger and will create a lot of gathers and bulk.

Instructions:

1 Prepare a pattern using the circle calculations. Using the pattern, cut two half circles from the knit fabric.

2 Place them with RST and pin the side seams. Sew with a ½" seam allowance, trim, and press.

3 Cut a band 3" wide and as long as the measurement for the inner circle and one inch for the seam allowance.

4 Place the short ends with RST and sew with a ½" seam allowance.

5 Fold the width of the band in half with WST. Pin and baste ¼" from the edge all the way around, leaving a 2" opening at the seam.

6 Fold at the seam and divide the band into fourths, marking with pins.

7 Divide the circle opening into fourths. Use the side seams as two of the markings and pin.

8 Align the seam in the band with one of the circle side seams and pin.

9 Match all the other pins in the band with the circle opening.

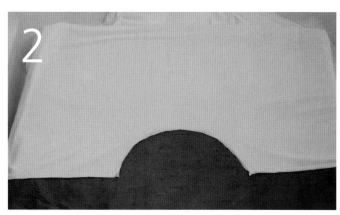

Pin two half circles RST.

Pin and baste.

10 Ease the circle fabric to fit the band, and pin.

11 Sew all the way around with a ½" seam allowance, except for the 2" opening in the band.

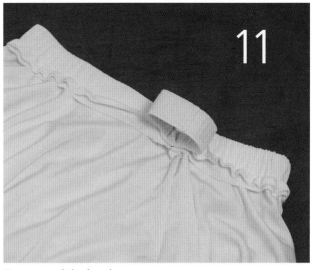

Sew around the band.

12 Place the safety pin at one end of the elastic and thread it through the band casing. Bring the safety pin to meet the other end of the elastic; overlap by ¼" and pin with the safety pin. Try the dress on to check the fit. Use a zigzag stitch to sew the overlapped portion of the elastic. Tuck the elastic into the casing, and sew the remaining 2".

13 Put the dress on, mark the hem, and trim. If you want the dress to puddle on the floor, allow for more length.

14 Serge the hem edge, or use the zigzag stitch to finish, or just leave the cut edge. For a curly edge, use the rolled hem feature on the serger, or stretch the fabric as you zigzag with a short stitch length.

Sash and Train

This sash can be tied over the bust for an Empire-style elegance, or go around the waist, tie in the back and be worn as a train. Use a sheer fabric with dots so that when some of it is used with the shrug, there will be a cohesive style.

Materials:

4 yd. sheer dotted organza fabric

White sewing thread

Tip:

For the sash, choose a fabric that doesn't fray when cut. A sheer organza or net with dots is a good choice.

Instructions:

1 Cut the sash/train the length of the fabric and 25" wide.

2 Fold the width in half with RST. Pin and sew the length with a ¼" seam allowance, leaving a 4" opening in the center. Sew the short ends.

3 Turn right-side out through the opening. Tuck the seam allowance inside the opening and slip stitch to close. Press.

Turn the sash right-side out.

Materials:

1½ yd. two-way stretch fabric

1½ yd. sheer dotted organza fabric

White sewing thread

Blanc de Blanc

The dimensions for the shrug will depend on your size, the fabric you select, and how long your arms are. The solution is to make a sample and alter to fit. If you are using an expensive fabric, make a sample in an inexpensive fabric with the same two-way stretch. Use the same fabric as the sash for the sleeve flounces.

Tip:

Select a fabric with a two-way stretch for the shrug. A sheer mesh with Lycra, a synthetic fabric with exceptional elasticity, is ideal. Some fabrics are best cut on the cross grain, while others should be cut on the grain line. You'll want the greater stretch across the back (length of shrug).

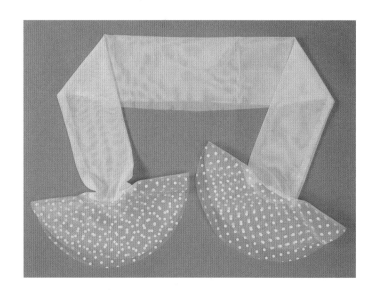

1 Cut a rectangle (using the basic chart below as a starting point), fold the width in half with RST, and pin.

2 Leave a center opening, which is determined by size, and sew from each side of the opening to the ends.

3 Cut two circles for the sleeve edge flounce. Divide into fourths and mark with pins. Refer to the flounce chart below, or create your own pattern.

4 Divide the sleeve edge into fourths and mark with pins.

Match the pins on the sleeve edge with the flounce and pin together. Sew with a ¼" seam allowance.

Tip:
If the sleeve opening is too large, consider tapering it in, starting from the sides of the center opening. Use a flounce with a smaller inner circle radius.

Tip:
To help you decide on the shrug size, determine the length and width needed.

The entire length of the shrug, including the flounce, goes from 2" below the wrist, across the back, to 2" below the other wrist. Get someone to help you with the measurement so you can keep your arms down at your side. The length without the flounce is determined by using the entire length measurement and subtracting the flounce. In this case, I had a finished 5" flounce length. So, add 5 to the length in the chart below to see if you need to make it longer or shorter.

Width: The width must accommodate the largest part of your arm.

Center opening: The center opening is determined by your shoulder and chest width. The center opening listed below is just a starting point. It will be best to baste the opening to that size, try it on, and then make adjustments.

Blushing Bride Hat and Veil

This chic hat is perfect for an altered style bride. Choose creamy feathers and a veil with tiny "scatters" for a unique look.

Instructions:

1 Cut from the edge of the circle to the center of the circle stabilizer. Overlap the edges 1" and sew or glue in place.

2 Pleat the short ends of the dotted veil to a width of 2" and sew the ends.

3 Pin the two pleated veil edges at the back of the stabilizer circle. Try on to see if the veil placement pleases you. To make the veil come down farther, place the ends closer to the sides of the circle. Hand sew in place.

Materials:

5" diameter circle of heavyweight stabilizer

½ yd. approximately 10"-wide dotted veil

1 yd. plain veil

⅓ yd. white feather boa

White sewing thread

Millinery glue

4 Evenly space, pin, then sew the edge of the veil to the circular edge of the stabilizer. Hand sew in place.

5 Tie a bow with the plain veil, and glue to the back of the circle.

6 Place the boa around the circle of stabilizer, covering the veil edges and curl the remainder inside the circle. When pleased with the placement, remove the boa, place glue on the circle, and carefully replace the boa.

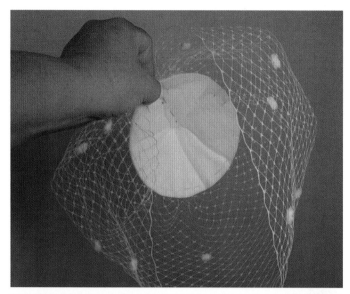

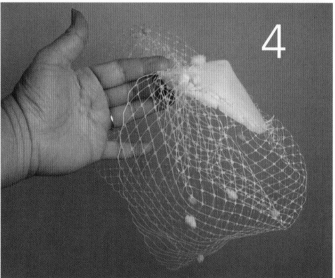

Sew the veil to the stabilizer.

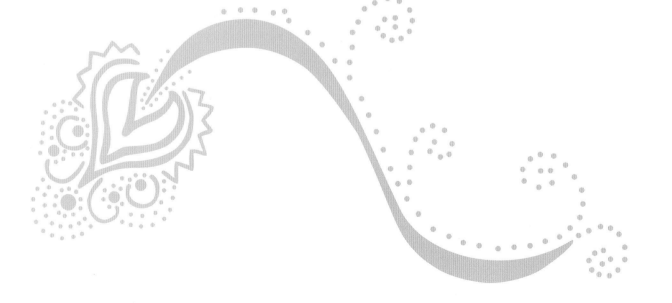

Heart's Desire Purse

This special accessory is the perfect
accompaniment with its heart-shaped frame,
white-on-white brocade and pearls. The chain
purse handle and tassel was created from an
extra-long chain necklace. The chain links were
soldered, which gave it the strength to use as a
handle. The chain is embellished with dangling
silver circles, which replicate the wedding ring,
and pearls that represent purity of love and
harmony.

The heart shape of the frame represents the
love of this special day. The jacquard design of
dragons woven into the fabric stands for the
longevity and fierce strength of the couple's
dedication. This is truly a special day.

Materials:

1 heart-shaped purse frame

¼ yd. white fabric

¼ yd. white lining fabric

2 small snap clips

White sewing thread

Clear polyester thread or clear
    beading thread

Long, embellished chain necklace

¼ yd. thin white batting (optional)

Instructions:

1 Using the pattern provided, cut two pieces out of the white fabric, batting and the lining. Place a layer of batting on the wrong side of the lining and treat as one.

2 Pin, then sew the pleats at the bottom of all four pieces as indicated on the pattern.

3 Place the two white fabrics with RST, and sew the sides and bottom with a ½" seam allowance. If the fabric ravels easily, sew another line of stitching right next to the first in the seam allowance. Trim and clip the curves.

4 Place the two lining fabrics with RST and sew the sides. Leave a 2½" opening in the center bottom.

5 Make a horizontal clip from the outside edge of the fabric to the end of the seam on each side (as shown with the dot). Do this for both purse sides.

6 Place the fabric purse inside the lining purse with RST and line up the sides seams.

7 Sew around the opening from seam to seam. Trim and clip the curves.

8 Turn right-side out through the opening in the bottom of the lining. Sew the opening closed. Tuck the lining inside. Press.

9 Place the purse behind the metal frame. Thread the needle with a double length of clear thread and tie a substantial knot.

10 Using a wire cutter, cut a length of chain to fit the heart shaped area with the holes. Use the method of sewing through the holes and capturing a bead, except in this case, sew through a chain link and send the needle back into the same hole. Continue in that manner.

11 Cut another length of chain for the strap. Place one snap clip on each end. Use the snap clip to attach the strap to the small loop area provided on the frame.

12 Optional: Create a matching tassel by cutting the remainder of the chain in similar lengths. Collect the centers of each strand and sew it to the center of the purse as shown.

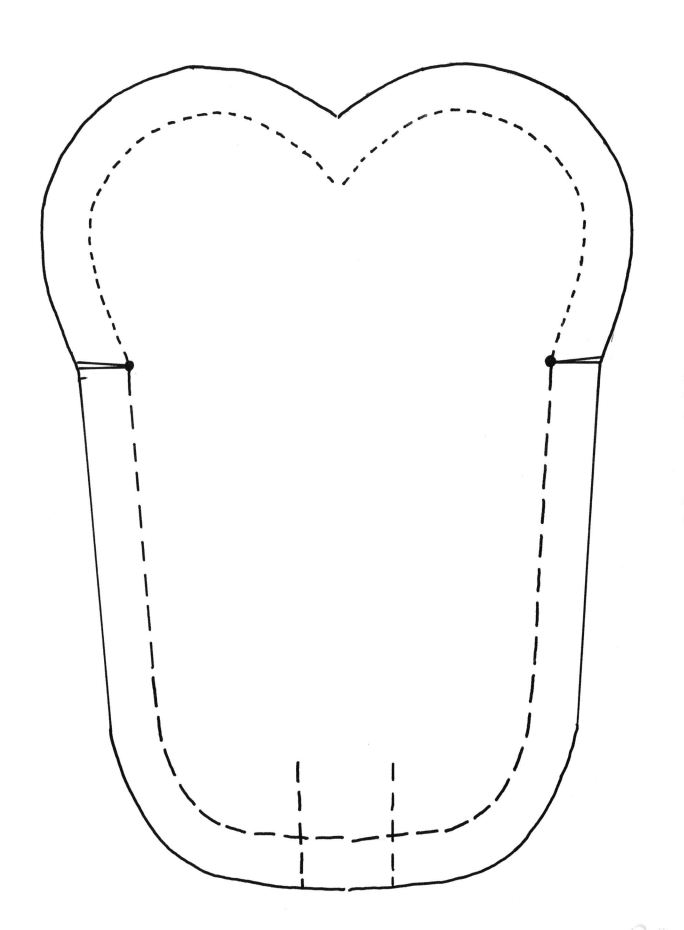

Glossary

Basting: Long, loose stitching by hand or with the sewing machine to temporarily hold pieces of fabric together.

Bias: A line across the grain at a 45-degree angle to the selvage. Cloth strips cut at this angle allow for stretch, ease and a smoother fit around curves.

Clip: To make small cuts into the seam allowance up to the seam line around a curve. For a concave curve, cut away triangular notches. Cutting the fabric away will reduce bulk.

Cross grain: The grain of the fabric going across the width.

Edgestitch: Stitching close to the edge of a fabric.

Feed dogs: The teeth on the throat plate of the sewing machine that moves the fabric along.

Fusible web with a release paper: An adhesive to bond porous surfaces with heat (fabric, craft fleece, leather).

Fussy cut: Cutting around intricate designs.

Gathering stitch: Two parallel rows of a longer length stitch (8 to 10 stitches per inch) sewn ¼" apart.

Hemstitch: Hand sewing that secures fabric to fabric in an almost invisible manner. Send the needle through the hem edge and pick up two threads, moving diagonally and sending the needle through the hem again and repeating the process.

Mylar template: Thin, heat-resistant plastic sheets used to create template shapes for appliqué quilting and other techniques.

Pinking shears: Scissors with blades that are sawtoothed. It creates a zigzag edge when cutting which reduces fraying.

Pivot: Leaving the sewing machine needle down in the fabric while raising the presser foot to turn the fabric and then continue stitching.

Quick-grab glue: A glue with a tacky feel that allows an instant bond.

Quilting tracing paper: A crisp tracing paper that falls away easily after stitching.

Raw edges: Unfinished, cut edges of the fabric

RST and WST: Right sides together and wrong sides together

Scant: A little less than the listed amount.

Seam allowance: The seam between the cut edge and the seam line.

Seam sealant: A liquid adhesive applied to the edges of fabric to prevent fraying.

Selvage: The finished edges on both sides of a length fabric to prevent unraveling. The grainline is parallel to the selvage. The selvages are removed before cutting the patterns since they can obstruct the weave close by. Sometimes the selvage has an unusual fringed edge in decorator fabric. Consider cutting it off carefully and using it as a matching trim.

Slip stitch: Thread the needle with matching thread and knot. Send the needle from the wrong side up at the fold (of fabric that is being attached) and take a stitch into the other fabric. Bring the needle back into the fold, next to the first, and pass the needle inside the fold to emerge ¼" to ⅜" away and repeat.

Stay stitching: A single line of stitching to stabilize the fabric and prevent stretching.

Thimble: A protective shield worn over the finger.

Tracing table: A light table consisting of a box that houses a light source topped with a clear top. This allows you to transfer designs through paper and fabric. Tracing tables are readily available in craft and sewing catalogs.

Resources

Dyes, paints and fabric markers

Dharma Trading
(800) 542-5227
www.dharmatrading.com

Tsukineko
(800) 769-6633
www.tsukineko.com
Wholesale only

Fabric and leather

Fabric.com
(888) 455-2940
www.fabric.com

G Street Fabrics
(301) 231-899801-231-8998
www.gstreetfabrics.com

High Fashions Fabrics
(713) 528-7299
www.highfashionfabrics.com

Metro Leather
(212) 629-4545

Nancy's Notions
(800) 833-0690
www.nancysnotions.com

Sewing Studio
(800) 831-1492
www.sewing.net

Silver Creek Leather Co.
(812) 945-8520
www.silvercreekleather.com
Wholesale Only

Thai Silks
(800) 433-4313
www.thaisilks.com
Vogue Fabrics
(800) 433-4313
www.voguefabricsstore.com

Purse components

M & J Trimming
(800) 965-8746
www.mjtrim.com

Purse handles and embellishments

Beautiful Buttons
www.beautifulbuttons.com
Wholesale only

Creative Crystal
Hot-fix crystals
(800) 578-0716
www.creative-crystal.com

Lacis
(510) 843-7178
www.lacis.com

Leisure Arts
(800) 526-5111
www.leisurearts.com

Sewing machines

Baby Lock
(800) 313-4110
www.babylock.com

Bernina
(630) 978-2500
www.berninausa.com
Brother
(800) 521-2846
www.brother-usa.com

Husqvarna Viking
(800) 358-0001
www.husqvarnaviking.com

Janome
(800) 631-0183
www.janome.com

Pfaff
(800) 997-3233
www.pfaffusa.com

About the Author

Stephanie Kimura is the designer and owner of a wearable and decorative arts pattern company. She is the author of *Bags With Style*, *Bags And Accessories With Style*, and *Art To Wear With Asian Flair*, published by Krause Publications. Her goal is to promote artful sewing and embellishment through trunk shows, lectures, demos, patterns and books, Visit her website, www.StephanieKimura.com, for more creative ideas.

Add Dazzling Personal Design to Your Wardrobe

AlterNation
Transform, Embellish, Customize
by Shannon Okey and
Alexandra Underhill

This is the indie-crafter's DIY fashion bible to personalizing wardrobes with a wide range of no-sew and low-sew techniques.

Softcover • 8 x 10 • 144 p
250 color photos • 10 b&w illus.
Item# Z0713 • $19.99

Transforming Fabric
30 Creative Ways to Paint, Dye, and Pattern Cloth
by Carolyn A. Dahl

Discover the secrets of dyeing, painting and patterning beautiful cloth with this inspiring guide. You'll discover background on techniques and lots of fresh ideas to ensure successful results.

Softcover • 8¼ x 10⅞ • 160 p
200 color photos, plus illus.
Item# TSFF • $23.99

Denim by Design
by Barbara Chauncey

Outgrown or outworn doesn't have to mean outdated. Transform recycled denim into dynamic clothing such as vests, purses, and more, using custom-fit techniques and embellishments.

Softcover • 8¼ x 10⅞ • 128 p
175 color photos
Item# Z1638 • $24.99

Bags and Accessories With Style
by Stephanie Kimura

Learn to apply Stephanie Kimura's unique contemporary style to more than bags, through 30 projects— including coordinated sets. Purses and belts to hats and shawls, it's in this fun guide to flirty designs.

Softcover • 8¼ x 10⅞ • 128 p
100 color photos, 50 illus.
Item# FACST • $22.99

My Style My Place
by Allyce King and
Nicole Thieret

Empower a young sewing sister to tap into her own individualistic and creative spirit and explore the possibilities of 25 quick do-it-yourself projects for the home and wardrobe.

Softcover • 8¼ x 10⅞ • 128 p
125 color photos
Item# Z0935 • $24.99

krause publications
An imprint of F+W Publications, Inc.

P.O. Box 5009, Iola, WI 54945-5009
www.krausebooks.com

Order directly from the publisher by calling
800-258-0929 M-F 8 am - 5 pm

Online at www.krausebooks.com, or from booksellers and craft and fabric shops nationwide.

Please reference offer **CRB8** with all direct-to-publisher orders.